D1402423

THE GOLDEN AGE OF
STEAM

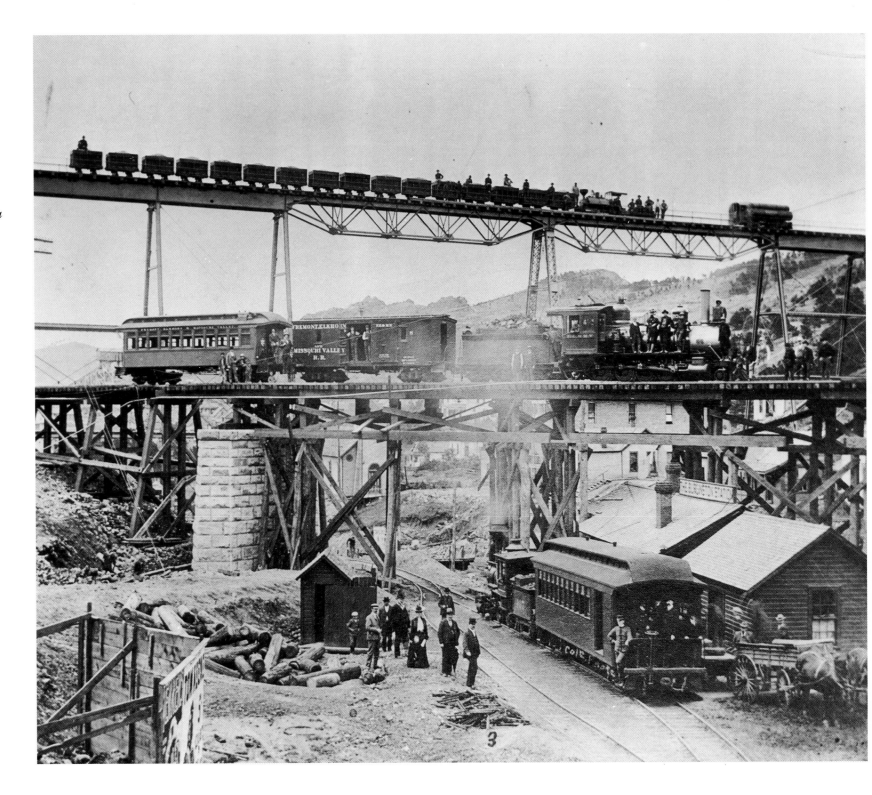

RIGHT: Three lines converge in western South Dakota in the 1800s. On top is a local mine railroad, in the centre is the Fremont, Elkhorn & Missouri Valley (a Chicago & North Western subsidiary), while below is a predecessor of today's Burlington Northern.

OPPOSITE: The Station, a painting by Frith from 1862.

THE GOLDEN AGE OF
STEAM

CHRISTOPHER CHANT

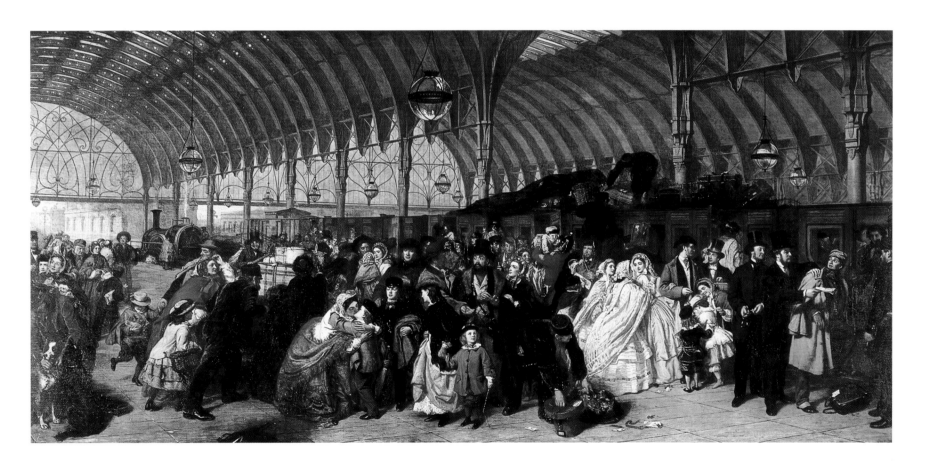

Copyright © Regency House
Publishing Limited

No part of this book may be
reproduced or transmitted in any form
or by any means electronic or
mechanical including photocopying,
recording, or by any information
storage and retrieval system, without
permission from the publisher.

This 2000 edition is published by
Gramercy Books™, an imprint of
Random House Value Publishing, Inc.,
280 Park Avenue, New York,
NY 10017

Gramercy Books™ and design are
trademarks of Random House Value
Publishing, Inc.

Random House
New York • Toronto • London •
Sydney • Auckland

http://www.randomhouse.com/

Printed in Hong Kong

ISBN 0-517-16164-8

10 9 8 7 6 5 4 3 2 1

*The Conestogo covered wagon
and the classic American
4-4-0 locomotive did more
than any other types of
transport to open up the West.*

The first train over the Missouri river on tracks laid on ice. March 1879.

Chapter One
A NEW CONCEPT IN TRANSPORT

The DeWitt Clinton, *built for the Mohawk & Hudson Railroad by the West Point Foundry, which made the 17-mile (27-km) trip from Albany to Schenectady in less than an hour.*

For more than a century up to the time of its disappearance from the tracks of the Western world in the period following World War II, the steam locomotive was redolent of the whole concept of mass transport for people and goods. In fact it was the invention and development of the steam locomotive that opened the period of mass transportation and, as a comparatively early product of the Industrial Revolution, made this revolution the truly huge phenomenon it became in pointing the way to the modern world.

The steam locomotive is based on the concept that water, when heated to a temperature above boiling point, tries to turn into steam and in the process expands in volume about 1,000 times. Kept inside the boiler, the steam is confined in volume and its pressure therefore increases, but once moved to a cylinder containing a sliding piston drives the piston along the length of the cylinder. This movement of the piston is translated to the wheels by a system of connecting rods attached to the driving wheels at a radial point well apart from the central axle, the pressure of the steam and the linear movement of the piston thus becoming the rotation of the wheels.

The steam locomotive is thus comprised of the two separate but mutually dependent elements of the boiler and the engine. The boiler is a closed unit which, in the case of most steam locomotives, also includes a rear-located firebox and a matrix of tubing to conduct the fire's hot gases through the boiler proper to a smokebox mounted at the opposite end of the boiler. A regulator valve (which is in fact the throttle), controls the release of steam into the steam pipe to the engine from which, after the extraction of most of its useful energy, it is removed by means of the blast-pipe into the smokebox and thence up the chimney. The departure of the steam from the blast-pipe lowers the pressure in the smokebox and so enhances the induction of more air to draw the fire in the firebox in a manner proportional to the amount of steam being used. This nicely balanced arrangement ensures that the more steam is used (and therefore needed), the more steam is made.

The fires of most steam locomotives are coal-burning, the fire burning on a grate of iron firebars through which the ashes fall into an ashpan. Other elements of the boiler include a method for filling the boiler with water (and then of replacing the water that

has been turned to steam and used before being exhausted) from a water tank that is fitted on the locomotive itself or on a tender towed behind the locomotive: a locomotive with onboard water tankage is a tank locomotive, while that with a towed tender is a tender locomotive.

The engine proper is based structurally on a number of frames fabricated from iron (later steel) plates or bars, or alternatively produced as a single casting. In this unit are the slots for the axle-boxes carrying the wheel sets, each comprising a pair of wheels on a single axle: the axle-boxes are attached to the frames by springs to provide shock absorption. Each

containing a single piston, the cylinders are attached to the frames, and the power generated by the movement of the pistons, as each of these is moved by the admission of steam into its cylinder (alternately at each end) is transferred to the wheels by a rod-and-guide system, this comprising a cross head and one or more guide bars. A piston rod connects the piston to the cross head by means of a steam-tight gland in the end of the cylinder, and a connecting-rod attaches the cross head to the driving wheels, with drive to other pairs of wheels possible by the addition of coupling rods.

A valve or valves are used to duct the

The locomotive Atlantic *with a pair of Imlay coaches, built for the Baltimore & Ohio Railroad in the 1830s.*

FAR RIGHT: A steam engine of James Watt's own design showing sun-and-planet gear converting up-and-down motion of beam to rotary motion for driving machinery. From a cigarette card published in 1915.

RIGHT: James Watt (1736–1819), Scottish engineer and inventor. From a chromolithograph published in London in 1824.

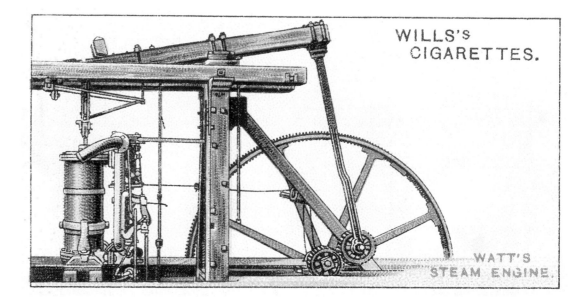

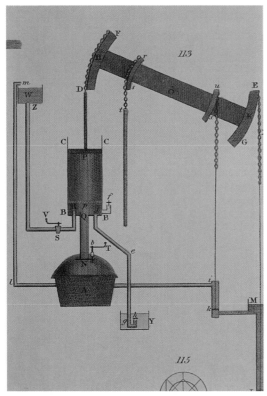

RIGHT: Thomas Newcomen's schematic engine. A colour print published in London in the early 19th century. Newcomen lived from 1663–1729.

steam into or out of the end of the cylinder when and (according to the direction and speed of movement) where it is required. These valves are linked with the wheels by means of valve gear. There have been many types of valves and associated valve gears, but all work on the concept that admission of steam into one end of a piston-fitted cylinder will result in movement of the piston with a force based on the pressure of the steam and the area of the piston head.

The start of the 19th century found steam well established as the fixed power source driving the Industrial Revolution, most notably in the steam engines designed by James Watt and Thomas Newcomen in the 1780s: these were low-pressure beam engines, and found their main employment in the pumping of water out of mines. These early steam engines were inefficient and also very heavy. Even so, far-sighted inventors were already at work trying to develop a steam-powered form of transport. Two of the earliest pioneers were James Watt and William Murdoch, who sought to exploit the possibilities inherent in steam power for the creation of a mechanical road carriage. Less far-sighted but eminently more practical was a Cornishman, Richard Trevithick, who appreciated that the best way to harness the power of current steam engines was in a locomotive for use on a wagonway, the type of simple cart-and-tack system used in European mines since the Middle Ages. From the 1790s Trevithick started the design of high-pressure steam engines offering a considerably better power/weight ratio than their predecessors. It is to Trevithick that

HOW TO INSURE AGAINST RAILWAY ACCIDENTS.

TIE A COUPLE OF DIRECTORS À LA MAZEPPA TO EVERY ENGINE THAT STARTS WITH A TRAIN.

NAVVY IN HEAVY MARCHING ORDER.

FAR LEFT: A cartoon from Punch *magazine, spring 1853.*

LEFT: Railway navvies were sent out to the Crimea to build a railway and to help with digging trenches. From Punch *magazine, January 1885.*

there falls the distinction of having built the world's first practical steam locomotive, which initially ran at Coalbrookdale in Shropshire in 1803. Trevithick's next steam locomotive was completed in the following year, and during trials on the tramroad of the Pen-y-Darren ironworks in south Wales showed itself capable of hauling wagons carrying 15 tons of iron. The third of Trevithick's engines was completed soon after this, and was the *Catch-Me-Who-Can*, a locomotive powered by a single vertical cylinder at the rear and demonstrated during 1808 near Euston in London: the trials of this pioneering locomotive were undertaken on a circular track pulling a single carriage.

Trevithick's steam engines were typically of the kind with a geared drive from a single front- or rear-located cylinder to smooth flanged wheels. The locomotives were in themselves moderately successful in the technical sense, but their development was to a certain extent a dead end given the Luddite hatred of the primitive wagonways on the part of ironworkers and others who feared for the loss of their jobs if horses were replaced by steam locomotives. Another adverse factor was the limited strength of current wagonways, which were therefore unable to carry the weight of the locomotive (derived from a stationary steam engine and therefore very heavy) without frequent breakages.

Whereas the iron industry of South Wales

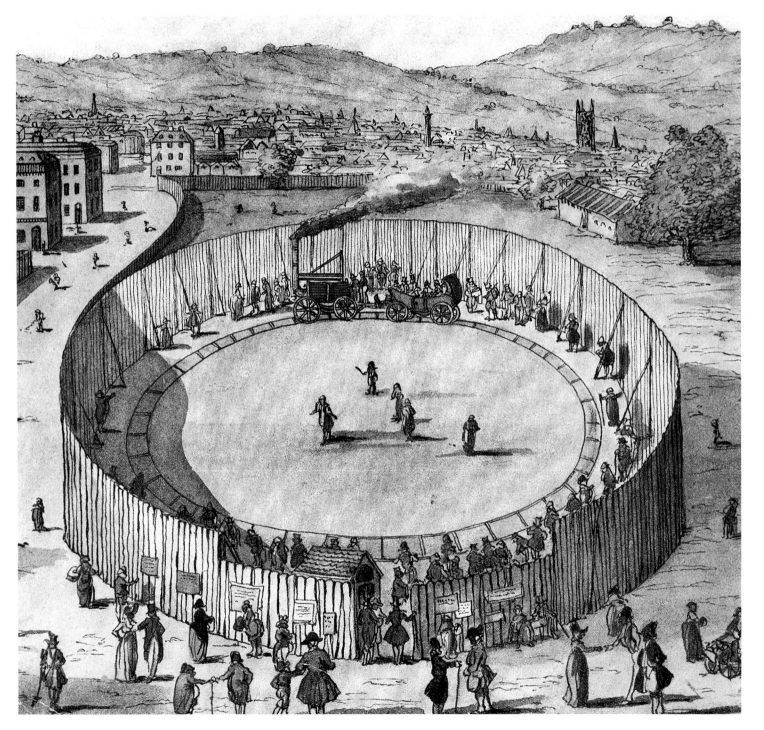

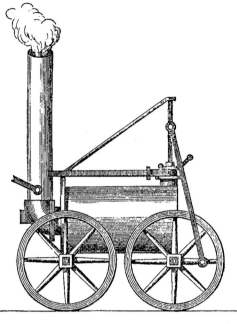

rejected the steam locomotive, the coal-mining industry of north-eastern England was more receptive to the concept. In 1812 the Middleton Colliery Railway started to use the world's first commercial steam locomotive, designed by Matthew Murray. This locomotive had two vertical cylinders and ran on strong cast-iron rails, one of which had a rack section engaged by a matching rack on the locomotive's geared driving wheel to provide maximum traction. By 1820 steam locomotives designed by Timothy Hackworth, George Stephenson and William Hedley were in service on the comparatively steep wagonways of the collieries at which these men were the chief engineers. Hedley's *Puffing Billy*, which was introduced in 1813, was a notable advance over its predecessors as

LEFT: Train crossing Chat Moss Bog. From T.T. Bury's Coloured Views on the Liverpool & Manchester Railway, *1831. The engineer was George Stephenson.*

OPPOSITE LEFT and RIGHT: Catch-Me-Who-Can, *a railway locomotive designed by Richard Trevithick. It was demonstrated in 1808 on a circular track near to where Euston Station in London now stands.*

ABOVE RIGHT:
Trevithick's Coalbrookdale
locomotive of 1803, a
museum drawing based on
an original contemporary
sketch. A single horizontal
cylinder, 4.75 x 36in (121
x 914mm), enclosed in a
cast-iron return-flue boiler
and provided with a
flywheel, drove the wheels on
one side only through spur
gears. Steam was
distributed through valve
plugs worked by tappets.
The cylinder was placed at
the same end of the boiler as
the furnace door and boiler
pressure was around
50lb/sq in (3.5kg/cm²).
There were cast-iron plate
rails, and axles were
mounted directly on the
boiler, without a separate
frame. There were no
flanges on the wheels.

BELOW RIGHT: Guyot's
Steam Carriage of 1769,
an example of an early
steam locomotive.

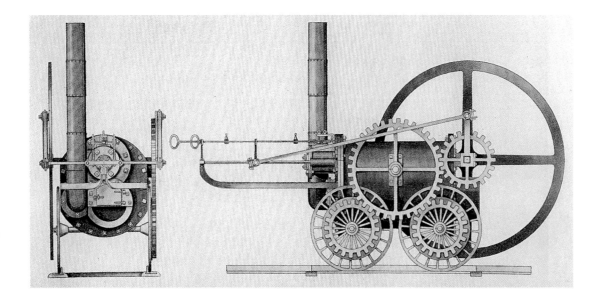

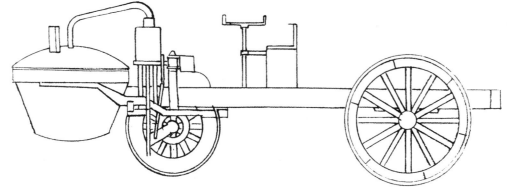

it was driven by a single crank on one side. As originally completed, the *Puffing Billy* had a 0-4-0 configuration, was then modified to 0-8-0 layout in an effort to cope more satisfactorily with poor track, but then reverted to its original layout. Hedley's next steam locomotive was the *Wylam Dilly*. Stephenson's 0-4-0 steam locomotive of 1815 for the Killingworth Colliery Railway in Northumberland ran on flanged wheels with

the driving wheels powered by two vertical cylinders operating a chain drive between the axles.

Even though these pioneering efforts had been undertaken on private railways designed solely for the movement of coal and some of the collieries' heavy equipment, the pioneers of the new science had in the process gained considerable design, manufacturing and operating experience. This proved invaluable

The graceful lines, sparkling paintwork and polished brass make this preserved Stirling 8-ft (2.4m) single-class locomotive a splendid sight.

opened the railway age in September 1825 by hauling a load of 68 tons along the 21-mile (34-km) track from Shildon to Stockton. There was enormous enthusiasm for the overall concept, but that people were not yet ready to entrust themselves to steam locomotion is shown by the fact that in its first eight years of operation the Stockton & Darlington Railway moved only coal and goods under steam power, people being moved in horse-drawn carriages.

Even so, George Stephenson must be regarded as the father of the railway. Despite the technical success of Locomotion No. I, the Stockton & Darlington Railway did not become the world's first steam-worked inter-city passenger line: as noted above, after the inaugural run passenger services reverted to horse power. So it was not until the opening of the Liverpool & Manchester Railway, in the course of September 1830, that the world's first genuine passenger-carrying railway came into existence. Designed by Stephenson, the Liverpool & Manchester Railway had to overcome considerable engineering difficulties, and made use of new and more

ABOVE: *George Stephenson's engine* Locomotion. *From Louis Figuier's* Les Nouvelles Conquêtes de la Science, *Paris circa 1890.*

RIGHT: *William Hedley's* Puffing Billy *(1813). From Amédée Guillemin's* The Applications of Physical Force, *London, 1877.*

when the world's first public steam railway was planned. The spur for this development was the need of local businessmen to move coal as well as goods between the mines in the south of County Durham and the port of Stockton on the River Tees. The local consortium employed George Stephenson as the chief engineer of the Stockton & Darlington Railway. Stephenson designed and supervised the construction of the track, and also designed and built the pioneering steam locomotive Locomotion No. I, which

Replicas of Stephenson's Rocket *and Peter Cooper's* Tom Thumb, *which was originally built for the Baltimore & Ohio Railroad in 1829.*

reliable steam locomotives, such as the *Rocket* designed by Robert Stephenson, George Stephenson's even more talented son.

Progress in the development of the boiler and steam engine in terms of efficiency and power was, naturally enough, the driving force behind the creation of the great steam locomotives in the golden age of steam, which may be regarded as the period between the success of the *Rocket* in the Rainhill trials of October 1829 and the end of World War II in 1945.

Although it was the Stephenson *Rocket* that secured victory over four other contenders (the *Novelty*, the *Sans Pareil*, the *Cycloped* and the *Perseverance*) in the Rainhill trials of October 1829 to select the locomotive for the passenger service soon to be inaugurated by the Liverpool & Manchester Railway, the steam locomotive actually used for this first service between two cities, which took place on 15 September 1830, was in fact the *Northumbrian*. This locomotive was better in several significant respects to the *Rocket*: it had, for example, a smokebox to gather the ashes drawn through the boiler tubes; it integrated the boiler with the water jacket round the firebox, creating for the first time the type of boiler that was to become wholly standard for steam locomotives; it had cylinders with their axes in an almost horizontal position rather than the ungainly angle of some 35° used in the *Rocket*

LEFT: *A replica of the* Northumbrian *at the Derby works circa 1930, built by Stephenson for the Liverpool & Manchester Railway in 1830. After the Rainhill trials in 1829, locomotive development was very rapid.*

OPPOSITE: *Replica* Planet *crossing Swithland viaduct on the Great Central Railway, England.*

and causing the locomotive to rock; the cylinders were installed in a readily accessible position outside the wheels; and finally a proper tender rather than merely a barrel on wheels was used.

Others of the features which had made the *Rocket* a success in the Rainhill trials were continued in the *Northumbrian* though on a stronger and larger basis. The multi-tube type of boiler, with many tubes rather than one substantial pipe to conduct the hot gases through the water in the boiler, was retained as it was now clear that the greater area of multiple small tubes provided superior capability for the heating of the water they contained, and so too was the blast-pipe to ensure the exhaust of the spent steam up the smokestack and thus create a partial vacuum at the forward end of the whole boiler arrangement to create greater draw in the firebox at the rear of the boiler. The *Northumbrian* possessed just two cylinders outside the frames and directly connected to the driving wheels in the pattern that rapidly

ABOVE: A very early open-topped passenger carriage, which would have provided an extremely uncomfortable journey.

ABOVE RIGHT: The locomotive Minnetonka *of the Northern Pacific Railroad, purchased in 1870 for use in construction work in Minnesota.*

RIGHT: George M. Pullman's first sleeping car, a remodelled day coach. Its first run was on 1 September 1859, from Bloomington, Illinois to Chicago, on the Chicago & Alton Railroad.

became standard for all but articulated steam locomotives.

These positive features in the design and construction of the *Northumbrian* cannot disguise the fact, however, that this locomotive had poor features. The most significant of these was the location of the two large driving wheels towards the front,

The first British monarch to travel by train was Queen Victoria who in a train such as this, made her first rail journey from Slough to London in 1842.

Interior of one of the earliest Pullman cars operated on the Union Pacific Railroad.

locomotive was in motion.

The *Northumbrian* is usually listed as a member of the Rocket class, a 0-2-2 type of which seven had been delivered to the Liverpool & Manchester Railway in 1829 and 1830. Those immediately following the *Rocket* were the *Meteor*, the *Comet*, the *Dart* and the *Arrow* with their cylinders almost horizontal, and it is also worth noting that the *Rocket* was soon altered to the same condition. The *Phoenix* and the *North Star* each possessed a smokebox, while the *Majestic*, which followed the *Northumbrian*, possessed all the new features.

The successor class introduced on the Liverpool & Manchester Railway from October 1830 was the Planet class to the revised 2-2-0 layout. The new type reflected the rapidly developing design concepts of the two Stephensons, and as such had two forward-mounted horizontal cylinders, which enhanced the locomotive's weight distribution, as well as the driving wheels at the rear under the firebox, whose weight now improved the locomotive's adherence to the rails. Another major improvement, introduced to eliminate the tendency of earlier locomotives to sway as the drive power switched from one wheel to the other, was the relocation of the cylinders inside the wheels to drive the axle by means of a double-crank. The Planet class was relatively successful and many of these engines, some of them with

requiring the positioning of the heavy firebox and the heavy cylinders at the rear, over the two small carrying wheels, where their weight was offset only by the relatively light smokebox forward of the driving wheels. This reduced tractive effort, a process increased by the action of the drawbar, which imposed a lifting force on the locomotive's front end.

Another problem resulted from the combination of outside cylinders and a short wheelbase, which caused the locomotive to sway directionally until it was revised with a longer wheelbase and the cylinders shifted to the front. Another failing in the *Northumbrian* was the lack of any effective means to reverse the drive while the

New York Central's Empire State Express *No. 999 hauls a single passenger car.*

four coupled wheels, were made by the Stephensons and also by other companies including, most importantly of all, Matthias Baldwin of Philadelphia in the United States, which during 1832 produced the *Old Ironsides*. This was the first full-size steam locomotive from a company that became the world's most prolific manufacturer of such engines, totalling some 60,000 over a period of 130 years.

In historical terms it was the Planet class that may rightly be seen as the steam locomotive that proved beyond doubt that the age of mechanical transport was safe and, more importantly, commercially viable. It was the success of the Planet class that in reality made the Stephensons wealthy men and led to their reputation as the practical fathers of rail transportation.

It was on 15 January 1831 that the first full-size steam locomotive manufactured in

23

RIGHT: A Chicago, Milwaukee & St. Paul early day coach. American cars had a central aisle and exit doors at each end

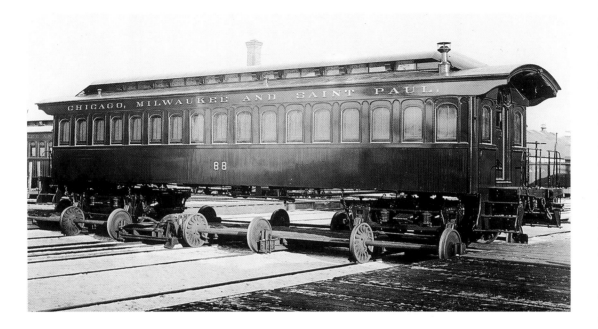

RIGHT: A passenger car built in 1873 by Jackson & Sharpe, predecessors of the American Car and Foundry Company.

the U.S.A. entered service. This was the *Best Friend of Charleston*, an odd 0-4-0 locomotive operating on the U.S.A.'s first commercial steam railway, the South Carolina Railroad. Made by the West Point Foundry in New York late in 1830 to the design of E.L. Miller, the *Best Friend of Charleston* had a vertical boiler, a well tank manufactured integral with the locomotive, four coupled wheels and two modestly inclined cylinders. None of the locomotive's features, except the coupled wheels, became standard, but the *Best Friend of Charleston* was nonetheless successful at the technical level and could pull five carriages, carrying 50 or more passengers at 20mph (32km/h). It was the explosion of the locomotive's boiler during 1831, after the fireman had tied down the lever controlling the safety valves to prevent the noise of escaping steam, that led to the universal adoption of tamper-proof safety valves to prevent any recurrence of this fatal incident. The locomotive was rebuilt with a new boiler and the revised name *Phoenix*.

More important than the *Best Friend of Charleston* was the *Brother Jonathan*, a 4-2-0 locomotive designed in 1832 by John B. Jervis for another American operator, the Mohawk & Hudson Railroad. This locomotive introduced the pivoted leading truck or bogie, which was derived from a notion that Robert Stephenson suggested to Jervis during a visit to England. Among its

features was a fairly small boiler, and volume for the connecting rods between the firebox and the main frames, which were outside the driving wheels, to the rear of the firebox. Only the four-wheel truck became standard to improve guidance round curves. The *Brother Jonathan* had a relatively long and distinguished career, in which it was later transformed into a 4-4-0 layout.

The Vauxhall-class locomotive, designed and built for the Dublin & Kingstown Railway of Ireland in 1834 by George Forrester, introduced two important features to the concept of the steam locomotive. The first of these was the installation of the cylinders outside the driving wheels in a horizontal position at the front of the locomotive, a location that made them effective and also left them readily accessible: in this arrangement the pistons and connecting rods powered the driving wheels by means of separate cranks on the outside of the wheels. The second important feature was the provision for the first time of an effective mechanism to reverse the drive, although the locomotive had first to be halted. By 1836 most of these steam locomotives, also sold to other railways in the U.K., had been altered from 2-2-0 to 2-2-2 layout to improve their running.

The first two locomotives made in Germany during 1816 and 1817 were unsuccessful, so it was December 1835 before

LEFT: This American car's central aisle allowed passengers to move freely: lighting was improved from the 1860s when kerosene lamps replaced candle-burning lanterns.

LEFT: A British Great Western Region Saint-class 4-6-0 locomotive heads a passenger train. Though the first locomotive appeared in 1902, 32 were built before being given the name 'Saint'.

Union Pacific No.9000, a Union Pacific-type 4-12-2 three-cylinder locomotive, built by the American Locomotive Company in April 1926. This was the longest non-articulated locomotive ever built and had a tender capacity of 15,000 gallons (67500 litres) of water.

the first successful German railway began services as the Ludwigsbahn in Bavaria, linking Nuremberg and Fürth. Herr Scharrer, the railway's promoter, first planned to buy equipment from Robert Stephenson, but then contracted with two citizens of Württemberg for the supply of equipment that they warranted the equal of any British items. The two men then moved to Austria-Hungary and more than doubled the price they wanted, so Scharrer returned to Stephenson for a 2-2-2 locomotive known as *Der Adler* (The Eagle) and possessing a number of features of the Patentee delivered to the Liverpool & Manchester Railway in 1834. The Patentee was a development of the Planet class with

LEFT: Poster advertising train tickets at Hornellsville for the Erie Railway.

LEFT: A number of South American railways bought locomotives and cars from the U.S.A. These two passenger carriages in Ecuador are typical.

The popularity of preserved steam locomotives has encouraged main-line railways to run a number of 'specials'. Here the Didcot–Derby passes Hatton North Junction in England.

improved axles and wheels. The success of *Der Adler* is attested by the fact that the Ludwigsbahn operation bought more locomotives of the same type, and that the original locomotive was used up to 1857.

Henry Campbell, the engineer of the Philadelphia, Germanstown & Norristown Railroad in the U.S.A., decided that there would be advantages to the combination of coupled wheels, as pioneered on the *Best Friend of Charleston*, and the leading truck as introduced by the *Brother Jonathan*: this would increase the adhesive weight of a locomotive that would be able to ride smoothly round curves on tracks that were often very irregularly laid. The result was the world's first 4-4-0 locomotive, which was

completed in May 1837 by James Brooks for service in the movement of coal from local mines, but in fact introduced the most celebrated of all passenger locomotive wheel layouts even though it was not in itself successful as a result of its distinctly poor ability to cope with vertical irregularities in the track.

During 1836 the Garrett & Eastwich company of Philadelphia received an order from the Beaver Meadow Railroad for a 4-4-0 steam locomotive. The company's foreman, Joseph Harrison, knew of the problems of the Campbell 4-4-0 but also remembered the success of the *Brother Jonathan* that offered far greater stability through its combination on each side of two driving wheels and the

pivoted leading truck, which provided a type of three-legged stability. Harrison now decided that stability could be improved by making the two pairs of driving wheels into a non-swivelling truck through the connection of the axle bearings on each side by a large cast-iron beam that was pivoted at its centre and connected to the locomotive's main frame by a large leafspring. This created a three-point suspension system for an eight-wheel locomotive, a system that fully solved the problem of running on rough tracks. Indeed, it was so effective that it appeared in steadily more sophisticated form for locomotives up to much later 4-12-2 units. The locomotive in question was the *Hercules*, whose success led to the sale of many basically similar locomotives to several railroads and the elevation of Harrison to a partnership in a firm that became Eastwich & Harrison as Garret left it at this time.

With William Norris's Lafayette class of 4-2-0 engines, first for the Baltimore & Ohio Railroad in 1837, the locomotive took a major step toward its definitive form. Norris had started to built locomotives in Philadelphia during 1831, initially in partnership with Colonel Stephen Long, but then started up on his own and in 1836

produced for the Philadelphia & Columbia Railroad a 4-2-0 locomotive called the *Washington County Farmer*. This was similar to the *Brother Jonathan* in having a leading truck but different in the location of its cylinders outside the wheels and frames, and in the location of the driving wheels ahead of rather than behind the firebox to boost the proportion of the engine's weight carried on them. The success of the *Washington County Farmer* caught the attention of the Baltimore & Ohio Railroad, which by this time had

expanded its network to the extent that could no longer be usefully operated by its comparatively primitive Grasshopper-class locomotives, so the operator contracted for a class of eight Norris locomotives. Delivered in 1837, the first of these was the *Lafayette* that was the railroad's first locomotive with a horizontal rather than vertical boiler, although this was used in combination with a circular-section firebox with a notably domed top. The class was very successful, offering higher performance and lower fuel consumption than

In poorer parts of the world, such as India and some South American countries, passengers can still look forward to extremely uncomfortable rail journeys.

earlier locomotives, in common with enhanced reliability and simpler maintenance. In 1837 Norris also completed a similar unit for the Champlain & St. Lawrence Railway in Canada, and this was the first modern locomotive to be exported from the U.S.A., the well proven capabilities of the type then combining with excellent gradient-climbing capability to secure a significant number of other export sales including a number to Europe, where the first customer was the Vienna-Raab railway, whose *Philadelphia* was shipped late in 1837. Other Norris locomotives went to railways in Brunswick, Prussia and the U.K. Such was the demand for Norris locomotives that the company found it commercially sensible to offer its type in four sizes and therefore weights differentiated by cylinder bores and grates of different sizes. The Norris type of locomotive was also widely manufactured in Europe, often without any form of licence.

LEFT: A Peruvian steam locomotive hauls a passenger train through mountains.

OPPOSITE: Cramped conditions are more than obvious in these open carriages of the Indian railway.

Chapter Two
STEAM LOCOMOTION COMES OF AGE

Here, circa 1895, Boston & Maine's American Standard-class locomotive No.150 has just moved out of the Danvers, Massachusetts engine house.

In Europe, meanwhile, momentous events in railway history had started to unfold with the appointment in 1833 of Isambard Kingdom Brunel as engineer of the planned Great Western Railway linking London with the west of England. Brunel was not a man to be impressed with current achievements, and one of his earliest decisions was that the gauge of the new railway was to be 7ft 0.25in (2.14m), which was the largest ever adopted for any railway, rather than the figure of 4ft 8.5in (1.432m) selected by the Stephensons and virtually standard in the U.K. Despite the grandiose nature of his plans and his manifest engineering genius, Brunel decided to take no close part in the ordering and design of the locomotives to pull the trains of the Great Western Railway, delegating these tasks to subordinates within the instruction that no six-wheeled locomotive was to mass more than 23,520lb (10669kg) and have a piston speed of more than 280ft (85m) per minute.

These limits made it impossible for the designers to create locomotives of any real significance, and there can be no doubt that the locomotives were the worst features of the Great Western Railway in its earlier days.

Supervising the locomotive fleet was Daniel Gooch, and it was only after a strenuous struggle with Brunel that Gooch was able to persuade the directors of the Great Western Railway to set in hand orders for more than 100 modern six-wheeled locomotives based broadly on the Stephenson Patentee type with layouts such as 2-2-2 for the 62 locomotives required for passenger services and 2-4-0 or 0-6-0 for the other locomotives that were used for freight services. By comparison with the free and easy situation in which most designers had worked up to this time, Gooch now worked within more tightly confined parameters, with the boilers, tenders, moving parts and many other components common to all the locomotives setting a good example of standardization.

Delivered in March 1840, the first of the new locomotives was the *Fire Fly* made by Jones, Turner & Evans of Newton-le-Willows

A Buddicom 2-2-2 at the Bricklayers' Arms Depot, London, 1951.

A German Class 01 4-6-2 steam locomotive, which headed the most important German steam trains of its day.

in Lancashire, and later locomotives of the same basic class were the *Spit Fire*, *Wild Fire*, *Fire Ball*, *Fire King* and *Fire Brand*. The capabilities of the new locomotive became clear on 17 March 1840, when the *Fire Fly* pulled a special train over a 30.75-mile (49.5-km) distance at an average of just under 50mph (80.5km/h) and reached a maximum speed of 58mph (93km/h). By the end of 1840 a further 25 of these locomotives were available. By December 1842 another 56 of the locomotives had been delivered by another six manufacturers, and the last of the series was not retired until 1879.

In 1841 there at last appeared in Germany the first indications that the local locomotive-manufacturing industry was starting to mature as three manufacturers each delivered their first offerings: these manufacturers were Borsig of Berlin, Maffei of Munich and Emil Kessler of Karlsruhe. At the time of Borsig's expansion from several other enterprises into locomotive manufacture, the Norris 4-2-0 type of locomotive was popular in European circles, and Borsig's first locomotives were 15 similar engines delivered to the Berlin-Anhalt railway company. Though based on the American original, the German locomotive had several Borsig improvements. The type was very successful and soon attracted additional orders. Within a period of two years Borsig had added further improvements, some of its own design and others derived from British ideas. The combination of an American basic design with German and British improvements created a highly attractive package, and was fully evident in the 2-2-2 Beuth-class locomotive of 1843. The equal spacing of the three axles offered a better distribution of weight than the Norris 4-2-0 type, and the new valves were so good that they became virtually standard for all steam locomotives over the next 60 years. The *Beuth* was the 24th locomotive manufactured by Borsig, and its success attracted a relative flood of orders to the extent that by 1846 Borsig had completed no fewer than 120 locomotives.

An exact French contemporary of the Beuth class was the Buddicom class of 2-2-2 locomotives designed for the Paris-Rouen

railway by W.B. Buddicom, one of many British engineers who took the ideas of the Stephensons round the world and, in this instance, also improved upon them. The Buddicom class was another step in the development of European locomotives from the *Northumbrian* toward what became established as the norm with two outside cylinders. The spur to the creation of the new design was the breaking tendency of the cranked axles of inside-cylinder locomotives:

as well as adopting outside cylinders, the Buddicom class also had the new type of Stephenson link motion and a deep firebox between the two rear wheels. The Buddicom class was very effective, and was built in moderately large numbers including 22 that were later converted to 2-2-2 tank locomotive standard.

During 1836 John Haswell travelled from Scotland to Austria-Hungary to supervise the entry into service of some locomotives bought

York station in England and the green and yellow livery of the North Eastern Railway, which ran fast trains from York to Edinburgh.

Union Pacific's locomotive No.574 (4-4-0) heading a passenger train at Genoa, Nebraska.

from the U.K. This task completed, Haswell remained in the country as the head of the locomotive element of the Vienna-Gloggnitz railway. Among Haswell's locomotive designs was the Gloggnitzer class of 4-4-0 units based on the Norris type but including unusual features such as the ability of the leading truck to move radially rather than just pivot round its centre as on the original Norris design, a change made desirable by the location of the coupled driving wheels close to the truck, which exercised a measure of constraint on the locomotive's axis and therefore made it important that the truck should possess a

measure of lateral displacement capability.

During 1855 Thomas Rogers of Paterson, New Jersey, built the *General*, which remains a classic example of the American Standard class of 4-4-0 steam locomotives, arguably the most numerous and successful locomotive design ever created. It was Rogers who was largely responsible for introducing in the U.S.A. most of the features that combined to make the true American Standard class. The most important of these was the Stephenson link motion, which permitted the expansive use of steam, and was used in place of the gab or hook reversing gears used up to that time

and provided only full forward and full backward positions. Rogers otherwise concentrated on good proportions and excellence of detail rather than innovation as such. To provide a measure of flexibility on tighter curves, early American Standard locomotives had the same type of flangeless forward driving wheels as their predecessors, but by the late 1850s the leading truck instead had provision for lateral movement to produce the same effect. The use of wood rather than coal was extremely common in the first part of the career of the American Standard locomotives, and as a result there were a wide assortment of spark-catching smokestacks in an effort to reduce the possibility of a spark flying off to the side of the track and setting fire to woods or crops. By the late 1850s, generally similar locomotives were being made by other manufacturers including Baldwin, Brooks, Mason, Danforth, Grant and Hinkley began producing similar locomotives, which generally operated on the roughly laid tracks of the period at an average speed of about 25mph (40km/h). The American Standard had a relatively long life: the need to pull longer and heavier loads meant that by the 1880s the original type had often been supplemented if not supplanted by larger steam locomotives using the same 4-4-0 configuration or alternatively the 4-6-0 layout. About 25,000 of these classic locomotives were built to a standard that was notable for its general uniformity in all but detail. The American Standard was the first and possibly the only universal locomotive, and the main difference between the units built to pull passenger trains and those intended for the freight market was the large diameter of the former's driving wheels, 5ft 6in (1.676m) as compared with the latter's figure of 5ft 0in (1.52m).

The Problem, or Lady of the Lake class of 2-2-2 locomotives, designed by John Ramsbottom and introduced to British service by the London & North Western Railway

during 1859, remained in useful first-line service for nearly 50 years, which was a considerable achievement in its own right and all the more so for a class introduced at a time that locomotive technology was still developing relatively quickly. The primary advantage enjoyed by the Problem class, as indeed with all of the great locomotives, was a total avoidance of complexity: the class had no trucks – for example, the leading axle being carried in the frames like the others, a very simple valve arrangement for the outside cylinders and, after the first ten, a simple injector system rather than pumps to top up

the boiler. One of the tasks entrusted to the Problem-class locomotives was the haulage of the Irish Mail between Euston in London and Holyhead on Anglesey, the locomotive being changed at Stafford. In 1871 Ramsbottom was followed by Francis Webb, an adherent of complexity. There resulted a number of complex and highly unreliable compound locomotives which were not as reliable as they should have been, and which led to a renewed demand for the services of the ageing Problem-class locomotives, which were largely rebuilt in the 1890s with greater weight in addition to the

The London & North Western (LNWR) Ramsbottom Problem 2-2-2 Prince Alfred at Bletchley station, Buckinghamshire, England, circa 1900.

The LNWR Ramsbottom Problem-class 2-2-2 Tornado at Carlisle, England in 1899.

crew cabs that had been added during an earlier rebuild programme.

Many French locomotive designs revealed a considerable measure of design flair, none more so than the 121 class that entered service in 1876 with the Paris, Lyons & Mediterranean railway. Needing locomotives more powerful than the Crampton 4-2-0 engines it was using at that time, the railway produced from 1868 some 50 long-boiler 2-4-0 locomotives and then, in the search for still more power for its service between the French capital and the Mediterranean coast, produced the 121 class of an initial 60 2-4-2 locomotives that had increased in number to 400 by 1883. All of the earlier long-boiler locomotives were then rebuilt to this standard for increased stability. Further improvement was introduced in 1888, when work was started on another batch of 2-4-2 locomotives, which must be regarded as one of the high points in French steam locomotive design. Only about one-tenth heavier than the original locomotives, these last engines introduced three definitive features in the form of the Walschaert valve gear (later standard all over the world), a boiler pressure almost two-thirds higher than that of the parent design, and a switch from simple to compound operation for much enhanced thermal efficiency to increase the ratio between the power produced and the fuel burned.

It had been a little disputed fact since the Patentee class of 2-2-2 locomotives that high speed demanded smaller guide wheels ahead of any locomotive's larger driving wheels, but in 1882 the London, Brighton & South Coast Railway introduced the Gladstone class of 0-4-2 locomotives. These were initially regarded with more than a touch of suspicion by the experts of the time, but experience soon showed that William Stroudley's decision to do away with guiding wheels was right, for the Gladstone-class locomotives ran perfectly and were also very attractive visually as well as comparatively cheap to run. Production of the Gladstone class amounted to 36 locomotives, the last of them completed in 1890, and the success of the type can be attributed mostly to its basically simple design, which resulted in good working and considerable reliability, and the careful arrangement of the suspension arrangements with leafsprings on the leading axle and more giving coil springs on the centre axle. Stroudley was not too strict an adherent to the concept of simplicity to use

Great Northern Railway's Stirling 8-ft (2.4m) single No.547, built in 1878. (Photographed circa 1905.)

complexity where this could offer advantages, and the Gladstone-class locomotives therefore included a system to condense the exhaust steam into the feed water, in the process recovering some of the heat that would otherwise have been wasted, and the use of air-driven assistance (using air from the Westinghouse air brake supply) for the screw reversing gear.

Designed by Daniel Gooch and introduced in 1888 on the wide-gauge lines of the Great Western Railway, the Rover class of 4-2-2 locomotives succeeded the Fire Fly class of 2-2-2 locomotives. The class's

prototype, in itself the result of a process of steady refinement, was the *Great Western* of 1846: this was in effect a stretched version of the Fire Fly class with greater grate area and tractive power brought by a one-fifth increase in weight. This was too much for the 2-2-2 layout and, after it had suffered a broken front axle, the *Great Western* was revised to a 4-2-2 layout with the leading pair of wheels supported by the frames rather than attached to a pivoted truck. There followed a series of steadily improved subclasses that provided the backbone of the Great Western Railway's fleet of locomotives.

RIGHT: The LNWR Webb
Teutonic-compound
2-2-2-0 No.1304 Jeanie
Deans.

RIGHT: The LNWR Webb
Teutonic-compound
2-2-2-0 No.1304 Jeanie
Deans.

RIGHT: Class D16/3
No.62618, resplendent in
fully lined apple green,
with the first British Rail
symbol (a very rare
combination), heads a
Cambridge train out of
Colchester, England in the
summer of 1950/51. One of
the last of the Claud
Hamilton class built by
LNER in 1923, it retained
the decorative valancing
when converted to a D16/3
in 1944.

From 1893 the Royal Prussian Union railway's S3 class of 4-4-0 steam locomotives pioneered a thoroughly modern look to Germany's rail network. The predecessors of the S3-class locomotive were a series of 2-4-0 locomotives that appeared in the 1880s with outside cylinders, but at this time there were passenger demands for higher levels of comfort and greater speeds, requiring the use of larger locomotives to provide the power required for what must inevitably be heavier trains. August von Berries, the superintendent of locomotives at Hanover, decided that the introduction of the larger boiler needed for additional power necessitated another axle to create the 4-4-0 arrangement that was so successful in the U.S.A. During 1890 the Henschel company manufactured two 4-4-0 locomotives with a two-cylinder compound-propulsion arrangement to a design by von Berries, and in the succeeding year Henschel constructed another four 4-4-0 locomotives (two each with compound- and simple-expansion propulsion) to the design of Herr Lochner, superintendent of locomotives at Erfurt. Lochner's simple-expansion system was deemed most effective, and there followed 150 locomotives before a reconsideration of the matter led to the decision that the von Berries type of compound propulsion offered advantages. During 1892 von Berries therefore designed an improved version of his original concept as the S3 design in which the letter stood for Schnellzuglokomotiv (express locomotive). The type was very efficient, and 1,073 such locomotives were made between 1892 and 1904, another 424 locomotives with smaller driving wheels being constructed as P4-class units.

The locomotive of the S3 class was notable not only for its considerable size, but also for its introduction of steam superheating. The attraction of superheating results from the fact that water evaporates to

expansion its presence in the cylinder is a waste, and so too therefore is the energy used to heat it in the boiler. However, the further heating of the steam after its departure from the boiler, and therefore no longer in contact with the temperature-limiting volume of water still in the boiler, allows the particles of water in the steam to be evaporated, in the process drying the steam and further increasing its volume. Additional heat raises the temperature of the dry steam, making it superheated. The slight cooling of superheated steam as it touches the walls of the cylinder etc. does not cause condensation until all the superheat has been removed. Superheating therefore removes the possibility of condensation in the cylinder, thereby allowing better use to be made of the energy locked into the steam's heat. The advantages of superheating had been appreciated for some time, but it was only in the 1890s that there appeared the first workable superheater designs, of which the most significant was that of Dr. Wilhelm Schmidt of Kassel. This was based on the ducting of the steam (between the boiler and the header that distributed the steam to the two cylinders) into a number of small tubes enclosed in a large-diameter tube through which flames from the firebox were ducted to create the superheating effect.

The Schmidt superheater was evaluated in single S3- and P4-class locomotives adapted in 1898 and proved generally successful except

The K4-class 4-6-2 locomotives were the mainstay of steam operations for the Pennsylvania Railroad until the end of World War II.

steam at a specific temperature dependent on the ambient pressure: at the 171-lb/sq in (12-kg/cm²) working pressure of the S3 class, this temperature is 376° F (191° C) and when there is water in the boiler the steam temperature cannot rise above that of the water. As the steam leaves the boiler it takes particles of water with it, and coming into contact with the cooler metal of the steam pipes, valves, cylinders and pistons it starts to lose it heat, part of it condensing into water to supplement the water droplets already being precipitated from the steam. Most of the work effected on the piston results from the expansion of the steam after the closure of the valve, but as water has no capacity for

A Pennsylvania Railroad 4-4-2, with slide valves, crossing the Skilkill river bridge.

for the distortion of the superheater's outside cylinder as a result of the great heat of the flames inside it. Schmidt therefore revised his concept to use the cooler but still high temperature of the smokebox, and this proved wholly successful. In 1899 two S3-class locomotives were completed with the definitive Schmidt smokebox type of superheater, and the success of the system was proved by a 12 per cent reduction in fuel

consumption. The system soon became standard for all new locomotives of the larger, high-speed type, further refinement of the concept resulting in fuel economies of up to 20 per cent. So successful were the superheated S3-class locomotives that 34 were still in service when the unified German rail network was created in 1924.

By the 1880s it had become clear that the movement of heavier trains at higher speeds

on the technically more advanced railways of the U.S.A.'s eastern states needed locomotives larger and more powerful than the American Standard type. The required type was created by turning the 4-4-0 layout into a 4-6-0 configuration by inserting a third coupled axle to the rear of the axles of the two standard pairs of driving wheels and streamlining the whole unit both internally and externally. These alterations were not without their problems, but even so some 16,000 such locomotives were manufactured in the period between 1880 and 1910. Typical of this impressive breed was the I-1 class made by the Brooks Locomotive Works of Dunkirk in New York during 1900 for the Lake Shore & Michigan Southern Railroad. The locomotives performed well, pulling heavy five-coach trains at moderately high speed with a smooth ride, including the classic *Twentieth Century Limited* de luxe service introduced in June 1902, but fell out of favour when the increase in passenger loads from the beginning of the 20th century required more power than could sensibly be delivered by an derivative of the American Standard class.

One of the most important operators in the U.S.A., the Pennsylvania Railroad had by the end of the 19th century become widely known for its large and powerful locomotives, most of them designed and built at the company's own facilities at Altoona. Typical of this breed were the 4-4-0 types of locomotive

No.2561 Minoru *on an East Coast express. England, August 1932.*

produced in several classes of which the most important and successful was the D16 class that first appeared in 1895 and was later recognized as one of the high points in the design and manufacture of American steam locomotives. The class was typified by large cylinders and a boiler that operated at a high pressure by the standards of the period, and it was also notable in purely visual terms for the considerable height of its boiler, which resulted from the installation of the firebox above rather than between the frames. The class was initially manufactured in two variants, namely the D16a class with driving wheels of 6ft 10in (2.032m) diameter for operation on the railway's flatter routes, and

the D16 proper with driving wheels of 5ft 8in (1.727m) diameter for operation on the railway's hillier routes. Some 426 D16-class locomotives were completed in five subclasses between 1895 and 1910. In the first years of the 20th century the locomotives of the D16 classes were generally outdone by the newer Atlantic- and Pacific-type locomotives in terms of power and therefore performance, but from 1914 just under half of the D16-class locomotives were considerably updated to the D16sb-class standard with a number of improvements including enlargement of the cylinders and a Schmidt-type superheating system. In this form the locomotives became important on branch lines, some of them

remaining in service until the early 1940s.

One of the key elements in the effort by the Atlantic City Railroad to wrest passengers from the Pennsylvania Railroad from the last years of the 19th century was the Camelback class of 4-4-2 locomotives, which had an unusual longitudinally-squashed appearance but introduced a number of important features. These last included a firebox that was both wide and deep, allowing the effective burning of anthracite coal and, as it was later found, bituminous coal and then oil. Other notable features were pairs of compound cylinders on each side with drive by means of a common cross head, and the camelback cab for the driver, who was thus carried over the

In their day, Claud Hamilton-class 4-4-0 locomotives were the expresses of the Great Eastern Railway.

boiler, while the fireman was provided with only the most rudimentary protection in the normal location at the rear of the locomotive. The arrangement certainly gave the driver a good field of vision, but made communication between the driver and fireman extremely difficult. At the technical level the Camelback class was successful, and was therefore built in moderately large numbers for the Atlantic City Railroad (soon the Philadelphia & Reading Railroad). Several other railroads on the east coast of the U.S.A. also built

locomotives of the same basic concept.

By the end of the 19th century the standard American locomotive was of the 4-4-0 configuration, but by this time it was clear that further progress in terms of hauling ability and speed demanded a configuration with more than eight wheels. So there appeared a number of 10-wheel designs divided neatly into the 4-6-0 and 4-4-2 layouts: the former provided greater adhesive weight (the weight on the driving wheels) but was limited by the area of the grate that could

be installed between the rear pair of driving wheels, while the latter (later known as the Atlantic type) offered lesser adhesive weight but could be fitted with a larger grate between the undriven rear wheels.

The Pennsylvania Railroad almost inevitably adopted the Atlantic type of locomotive as it already possessed the network of heavier track capable of accepting this type's heavy axle loads, and at the technical level wanted to be able to burn large quantities of modest-quality coal rather than smaller quantities of high-grade coal. Made at the railroad's Altoona facility in 1899, the first two Atlantic-type locomotives had a grate area of 68sq ft (6.32m²), which was more than twice the figure for any of the railroad's 4-4-0 locomotives. A third locomotive had the smaller grate area of 55.5sq ft (5.16m²), and it was this size that became standard for all later Atlantic-type locomotives, which totalled 576 in a number of subclasses. By 1913 manufacture of the Atlantic type had reached 493 units, and it seemed that the type had reached the limit of its development in the face of competition from the more modern Pacific type with its three pairs of coupled driving wheels. It was just before this stage that Axel Vogt, the railroad's chief engineer, decided that the driving wheel arrangement of the Pacific type was unnecessarily complex and planned a further improved version of the Atlantic type with a boiler increased in maximum diameter from 5ft 5.5in (1.664m) to 6ft 4.75in (1.949m) and with a combustion chamber at the front. The prototype of this E6 class of locomotives first appeared in 1910 and revealed greater power than the Pacific type at higher speeds. Two more locomotives were then made with a superheating system, allowing a further increase in cylinder diameter, and these locomotives displayed very good performance. There followed 80 E6-class locomotives all completed between February and August

1914 to become the mainstays of the Pennsylvania Railroad's express services on flatter parts of its route network. After the advent of the definitive K4 class of Pacific-type locomotives after the end of World War I in 1918, the E6-class locomotives were gradually relegated to lesser services. Many of the earlier locomotives were upgraded over the years with features such as superheating, five of them remaining in service to 1947.

In Europe, January 1900 witnessed the appearance of the first Claud Hamilton-class 4-4-0 locomotive, named for the chairman of the Great Eastern Railway. Although its inside-cylinder layout was typical of practices

in the previous century, forward-looking features were evident in the large cab with big side windows, power-operated reversing gear, water scoop, and provision for the burning of waste oil products (a by-product of the company's oil-gas operation) rather than coal. Good features that were not quite as advanced were an exhaust steam injector and a variable-nozzle blast pipe. The history of the Claud Hamilton class was complex, and eventually extended to cover a total of 121 locomotives manufactured between 1900 and 1923 in a number of subclasses characterized by features such as larger boilers, a superheating system, and piston rather than slide valves. All these features were built into the definitive Super Claud class of which 10 were completed. As new-build locomotives introduced improved features, most of the older units were rebuilt to the improved standard, most of them by the London & North Eastern Railway that introduced its own designation system. In overall terms, therefore, there were 41 of the original Claud Hamilton (LNER D14)-class locomotives that served up to 1931 and underwent no rebuilds, 66 of what later became the D15 class (nine rebuilt) that served between 1903 and 1933 and introduced the Belpaire firebox, four of what later became the D15/1 (70 rebuilt) class that served between 1911 and 1935 and introduced the superheating system, none of what became the D15/2 class (80 rebuilt)

Norfolk & Western Railroad J-class 4-8-4 No.609 on a westbound passenger train.

Western Railway's Dragon *locomotive.*

included inside low-pressure cylinders located in line with the forward axle of the leading truck and powered the leading coupled axle, and outside high-pressure cylinders installed in the standard position above the rear axle of the leading truck and powered the rear pair of coupled wheels. The de Glehn Atlantic-type locomotives were used for services such as the boat trains between Paris and Calais on some of the hardest schedules in the world, but the long-term performance of the locomotives was remarkable. The type offered very low specific fuel consumption and considerably eased the task of the firemen who had to shovel coal into the fire.

So successful was the de Glehn Atlantic type that orders were placed for an additional 152 locomotives including 59 for four other French operators, 79 for the Royal Prussian Union railway in Germany, and the other 14 for operators in Egypt, the U.K. and the U.S.A. Some of these later locomotives were completed to slightly different standards, notable mainly for their greater sizes, and the technical success of the de Glehn and du Bousquet compound-expansion system led the French railways to keep the system for many later classes of 4-6-0, 2-8-2, 4-6-2 and 4-8-2 locomotives.

During 1901 there appeared the first of probably the single most famous type of express passenger locomotive ever constructed, a type that was built right to the

that served between 1914 and 1952 and introduced a lengthened smokebox, 10 of the Super Claud or later D16/1 class (five rebuilt) that served between 1923 and 1934 and introduced a larger boiler, none of the D16/2 class (40 rebuilt) that served between 1926 and 1952 and were basically similar to the D16/1-class units, and none of the D16/3 class (104 rebuilt) that served between 1933 and 1958 and saw the removal of the coupling rod splashers and the reintroduction of round-topped boilers.

Becoming chief engineer of the Société Alsacienne de Constructions Mécaniques

during the 1870s, Alfred de Glehn was responsible, together with Gaston du Bousquet of the Nord railway, for one of the classic compound-expansion systems for locomotives: indeed, most 20th-century express passenger locomotives were of the de Glehn compound type. De Glehn and du Bousquet initially collaborated on compound 4-4-0 locomotives introduced in the 1890s, but their best claim to fame was the Atlantic-type 4-4-2 class that appeared in 1900 as the first engine of 32 such locomotives for the Nord railway. The locomotives were aesthetically very attractive, and key features

locomotives not being retired until 1957.

During 1902 the Chesapeake & Ohio Railroad accepted its first Pacific-type locomotive, which was the initial unit of the F15 class, and in the process gained the distinction of introducing the truly definitive type of steam locomotive to American passenger services. The locomotive still possessed strong affinities with the past and had no superheating system, but was marked as something notably different from earlier types by its size and power. The first F15-class locomotive was followed by another 26 units in the period up to 1911, and the overall success of the type is attested by the fact that virtually all of the locomotives survived in useful service until the Chesapeake & Ohio Railroad switched to diesel locomotives in the 1950s. In the later stages of their career of 50 or so years, the F15-class locomotives were gradually relegated to less important services or to lines whose bridges could not support the weight of later locomotives, and a number of upgrades were effected to incorporate features such as Walschaert valve gear, a superheating system and a mechanical stoking system as well as improved cabs and, in some cases, new cylinders and even new frames. The success of the Pacific type of steam locomotive in service with American railroads was reflected in the subsequent manufacture of some 7,000 units of the same basic type for a host of operators, and the spawning of a

Locomotive No.2926, Saint Nicholas, *a member of the Saint-class of locomotives built for the Great Western Railway between 1902 and 1911.*

end of the steam locomotive era. In New Zealand A.W. Beattie, the chief engineer of the Government Railways, felt that the country's railway system needed a locomotive with a big firebox able to burn the poor lignite coal produced at Otago on South Island. Although Baldwin, the U.S. manufacturer selected for the task of designing the new locomotive, recommended a Camelback 4-6-0 locomotive with a substantial firebox above the rear wheels, Beattie wanted a 4-6-0 development with the firebox carried by a two-wheel pony truck to create a 4-6-2 configuration. The 13 engines were quickly completed and despatched across

the Pacific ocean in a process that created the generic name of the Pacific-type locomotive that was to be built in very large numbers in the years to come. The Pacific-type locomotives of the Q class also had the classic Walschaert type of valve gear (designed during 1844 by the Belgian engineer Egide Walschaert), and lacked only two features that were added in later locomotives to create the fully definitive Pacific-type steam locomotive: these features were a superheating system and inside admission piston valves in place of outside valves. After the implementation of some minor modifications, the locomotives of the Q class gave long service, the last of the

No.4079 Pendennis Castle, photographed in 1967.

number of derived versions for service with the Chesapeake & Ohio Railroad. These derivatives included the F16 class of 1913 with a larger grate area and a boost in tractive effort of almost 35 per cent, the F17 class of the following year with still further increases in grate area and tractive effort, and then in the period after the end of World War I the F18 and F19 classes with large 12-wheel tenders carrying increased volumes of water.

The type which introduced the large boiler with a wide firebox to British practice, the Large Atlantic class of 4-4-2 locomotives was designed by Henry Ivatt and built to the extent of 94 units between 1902 and 1910

for the Great Northern Railway at its own facility in Doncaster in southern Yorkshire. The class was unchallenged on the southern portion of the service between London and Edinburgh up to 1921, but was then replaced by 4-6-2 locomotives. Thereafter the type was still used for a number of celebrated but lighter services, and finally disappeared from service only in 1950. In common with most of the world's truly great locomotives, the Large Atlantic class was basically simple in mechanical terms but wholly modern in the features that truly counted. The cylinders were outside, the valves and valve gear were inside, and while the first 81 locomotives of

the class lacked a superheating system and possessed balanced slide valves, the final 10 had a superheating system and piston valves: superheating was later retrofitted to the earlier locomotives, most of which were also adapted to piston valves.

By the end of the 19th century, George Jackson Churchward, eventual successor to William Dean as the chief engineer of the Great Western Railway, had seen that his company's success demanded a virtually complete replacement of locomotive stock to provide a combination of greater homogeneity and superior performance. A first result of this thinking was the appearance during 1902 of the Dean (later William Dean) class of 4-6-0 locomotive. This seemed somewhat apart from the main stream of British locomotive thinking, but this was hardly remarkable given the close working relationship of Churchward and A.W. Gibbs, a senior engineer of the Pennsylvania Railroad in the U.S.A. The new locomotive can therefore be seen as a combination of American 10-wheel design thinking and British engineering practice: the American 10-wheel configuration was combined with cylinders and valve chests located outside the frames for maximum accessibility, and Stephenson valve gear inside the frames to drive the inside admission valves. Other American features were the cylinders and the smokebox, but most of the rest was of

1911 25 examples of the derived Court subclass with a superheating system installed from the beginning together with a number of further improved features, including a slight increase in cylinder diameter. One of the most important keys to the success of the Churchward locomotives was the designer's superlative Boiler No. 1 (including a system to clean and warm the water before it reached the boiler), which was used in the 77 units of the Saint class and also in 74 Star 4-6-0, three Frenchman 4-4-2, 330 Hall 4-6-0, 80 Grange 4-6-0, and 150 28XX 2-8-0 class locomotives.

Over the years, all of the Saint-class locomotives but the prototype were upgraded to the definitive standard typical of the last units to be completed. It is also worth noting that another 330 locomotives were built to a standard described as the Hall class, which differed from the Saint class mainly in having driving wheels with a diameter of 6ft 0in (1.828m) rather than 6ft 8in (2.045m) for greater tractive effort with little reduction in maximum speed.

British in concept but designed and manufactured for service hauling main trains in India, the BESA class of 4-6-0 locomotives entered service in 1905 and later production examples of the type are still in effective service on the Indian railway system. The Indian rail network at the beginning of the 20th century represented a combination of private enterprise under a system that gave the

The No.5029 Nunney *Castle.*

orthodox British concept. With steady refinement incorporated, this combination of American and British features became standard for the 2,000 or so locomotives of the classes designed under the supervision of Churchward and his immediate successors. Churchward's thinking was not inflexible, though, and it should be noted that it took him a considerable time to decide whether the advantage lay with the two-cylinder Saint class of 4-6-0 locomotives derived from the Dean prototype or with the four-cylinder Star class of 4-6-0 locomotives. Some 77 and 60 of these two classes were built, and it was not long before his retirement in 1921 that

Churchward finally preferred the latter.

The Saint-class designation was used for the two-cylinder Churchward 4-6-0 locomotives only after the completion of 32 units including three prototypes. The 19 units of the first batch were delivered in 1905, and some of them operated for a short time in a 4-4-2 configuration. The second batch of 10 units was delivered from 1906, and the first of this batch was also the first British locomotive with the Schmidt type of superheating, such a system later being retrofitted to the earlier locomotives. From 1907 there followed 20 examples of the genuine Saint class with a number of improved features, and finally from

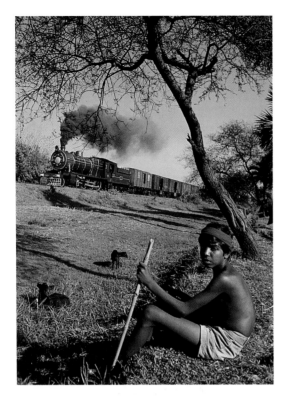

RIGHT: A BESA-class 2-8-0 hauling freight in India.

production of a larger number of types.

There were therefore Standard Passenger 4-4-0, Standard Goods 0-6-0, Heavy Goods 2-8-0 and Heavy Passenger 4-6-0 locomotives for the broad-gauge part of the system, which had a gauge of 5ft 6in (1.68m). All of these standard designs remained in service virtually to the present, and the BESA class was of the Heavy Passenger type. The first BESA-class locomotives were superbly engineered, and when introduced were larger and more powerful than virtually any other locomotives in the Indian subcontinent. The design was essentially a derivative of the 4-6-0 locomotives produced from 1903 for the South Western Railway by the North British Locomotive Company of Glasgow, which was

later supplemented in the BESA programme by Vulcan Foundry, Robert Stephenson & Company, Kitson, and William Beardmore in the U.K., while numbers were also produced in India as that country's industrial base became capable of the task.

The first examples of the BESA-class locomotive had no superheating system, outside cylinders, inside slide-valves and Stephenson valve gear. However, this initial standard was soon upgraded to an improved pattern with outside Walschaert valve gear, outside piston valves and a superheating system.

Back in Europe, the beginning of the 20th century was marked, as far as the Prussian state railway system was concerned,

government a measure of control in return for a guaranteed return on the operator's investments. This was a highly beneficial system for all concerned and, after the relative fiasco of the first stages of Indian railway development, in which gauges proliferated as a result of inadequate overall controls, marked the beginning of a more organized nationwide rail system. This process involved the establishment of a number of standard locomotive designs in a process that reflected the appreciation of British locomotive manufacturers that greater profitability resulted from the mass production of a few standard types rather than the penny packet

RIGHT: A BESA-design SP 138 (KS 1921) at Jam Sahib, the Borridge Special from Mirpur Khas to Nawabshah.

by the need to decide whether the superheating system was an alternative to the compound-expansion system or just an add-on element. The railway had built both simple- and compound-expansion locomotives since 1884, the former being used mainly for secondary routes and services, and the latter for primary routes and express services. The railway continued with the manufacture of non-superheated compound-expansion locomotives right up to 1911, but during this period also brought into service a number of simple-expansion locomotives with a superheating system, typical of the type being the P6 class of 2-6-0 locomotives, of which some 272 were delivered between 1903 and 1910. The two main problems with the P6 class were poor weight distribution and driving wheels with the small diameter of 5ft 3in (1.60m), which reduced speed to a figure below that now desired. In 1906 a class of 4-6-0 locomotives with a driving wheel diameter of 5ft 9in (1.750m) made its appearance with the object of allowing a speed of 68mph (110km/h). The early locomotives were unreliable, however, and their tendency to suffer mechanical failures made them very unpopular. A cure of the class's main difficulties was found in an alteration of the weight distribution and a reduction in cylinder diameter, but at the same time the railway authorities came to the conclusion that as the motion and valve gear were unsuitable for

speeds more than 62mph (100km/h), the engines should be used for secondary passenger and mixed-traffic services. This revised type was the P8 class, which had initially been schemed for express passenger work on a limited part of the Prussian system but now became history's most widely used and popular mixed-traffic locomotive.

The P8 class was essentially simple in concept and possessed a pleasing look with a round-topped boiler and a narrow but lengthy firebox. At least two other boiler types were later installed, but these did not change the locomotive's lines. The locomotive had a Schmidt superheating system, and the combination of a superheating system and piston valves with Walschaert valve gear provided the locomotive with one of the very highest levels of efficiency achieved in a simple-expansion engine. Almost inevitably there were a small number of teething problems with the P8 class, but once these problems had been eliminated the type was made in large numbers as its modest axle load allowed the operation of the type over most of the Prussian rail network. The P8-class locomotive was also constructed in small numbers for the railways of Baden, Mecklenburg and Oldenburg states in Germany, and also for export. Though supposedly a locomotive for secondary passenger services, the P8-class locomotive was used for primary passenger services in which

there was no requirement for a speed of more than 62mph (100km/h).

By the end of World War I some 2,350 P8-class locomotives had been manufactured for the Prussian railway network, but 628 of these had then to be handed over to other countries as part of Germany's war reparations. The Germans partially offset the loss of so many P8-class locomotives as war reparations by the construction of more locomotives of the same type, the last of which was delivered in 1928. With the creation of the German state railway organization the P8 class became the 38 class. Most of these locomotives were later fitted with new boilers, and their appearance was changed by the addition of feed water heaters, full-depth smoke deflectors and other outside features. During World War II the P8 class was soon to be discovered in the areas seized by Germany, most notably Poland, the western U.S.S.R., Czechoslovakia, Yugoslavia and Greece. Many of the class remained in these countries as Germany's eventual defeat unfolded, and in some of these countries the surviving P8-class locomotives were taken in hand for limited modification to bring them into line with national systems. German production of the P8 class of locomotives eventually totalled 3,438 units, and about 500 more basically identical engines were constructed in other countries including Poland, which also created 190 examples of a derived type with

LEFT: A P8 working in Romania. German-built locomotives were exported throughout the eastern bloc.

a larger boiler and wider firebox on the chassis of the P8 class. Some 2,803 examples of the P8 class survived to the end of World War II in Germany. The creation of different rail networks in the western and eastern parts of Germany, which later became West Germany and East Germany, meant that the available P8-class locomotives were, like other surviving engines, divided between the two networks. Both generally replaced the full-depth smoke deflectors with a more modern type, and some of the East German locomotives were

fitted with revised exhausts. The P8 class did not survive very long in West German service, for the adoption of diesel locomotives was followed through with some speed, and by 1968 there were only 73 P8-class locomotives, most of them working in the south of the country, where the last of them survived to 1973 as a result of the slowing of the replacement programme. This meant that the P8 class ultimately survived longer in West than East Germany, where the final units of the class were withdrawn from service in

1972. This was not the end of the line for the P8-class locomotive, however, for several units remained in useful service into the late 1970s in Poland and Romania.

Almost certainly the type that should be regarded as the finest example of the elegance associated with the golden age of steam locomotion, the Cardean class and related 4-6-0-type locomotives of the Caledonian Railway marked a genuine high point in steam locomotive design, construction and operation. Designed by John Farquharson

OPPOSITE: The Sir William Stanier *at Crewe North, England, 8 April 1962.*

The King George V
(*No.6000*).

McIntosh, the five Cardean-class locomotives were constructed at the Caledonian Railway's own St. Rollox facility and entered service in 1906. The design was decidedly conservative at the technical level, and as such reflected the belief of McIntosh that the improved ride and lines resulting from the installation of the cylinders and motion inside the frames offset the disadvantages of this arrangement's poorer levels of accessibility and the higher cost of crank axles. A superheating system was added to the locomotives in 1911 and 1912, and at a later time the Caledonian Railway, itself an air brake operator, ordered the addition of vacuum brakes so that other

companies' vacuum-braked trains could be hauled. Other features of the design were a steam servo-mechanism for the reversing gear, and a large bogie tender for longer non-stop journeys.

The French 4500 class of 4-6-2 locomotives of the Paris-Orléans railway, designed in 1907, has every claim to being not just one of the classic types of steam locomotive, but possibly the single most classic locomotive for express passenger train haulage. The 4500-class locomotive was the first Pacific type to enter service in Europe, and in its time was the most powerful and also the most efficient Pacific-type

locomotive of European origin. Added to this, the 4500-class locomotive was also very pleasing in appearance. Its one failing was a comparatively high level of mechanical complexity. Production of the 4500-class locomotives between 1907 and 1910 totalled 100 units including 30 made in the U.S.A., but there were also 90 examples of the 3500-class locomotive manufactured between 1909 and 1918 to a standard that differed from that of the 4500 class only in having a driving wheel diameter reduced by 4in (100mm). All 190 examples of these two classes were of the four-cylinder de Glehn compound-expansion type, and with an unusual grate wide at the back but tapering to a narrow front between the frames. Later units were completed with a superheating system, and such a system was then retrofitted to a number of the earlier locomotives. Another feature was the use of piston valves in the high-pressure cylinders but balanced slide valves in the low-pressure cylinders.

The technical limitations of the 4500 class started to become apparent after the end of World War I, when the rebuilding of France's infrastructure saw the replacement of the pre-war type of wooden carriage by a stronger, more durable but also somewhat heavier type of steel construction. André Chapelon, an engineer of the Paris-Orléans railway, suggested in 1926 that the locomotives should be cycled through a relatively major reconstruction programme, which in fact began only in 1929. The rebuilding of the 4500-class locomotives resulted in the creation of one of the definitive steam locomotive classes. Power production per unit of steam was increased by 25 per cent, while boiler improvements allowed the generation of more steam and thereby made feasible an 85 per cent increase in available horsepower. This transformation resulted from Chapelon's close analysis of the locomotive's entire operating cycle, resulting in an appreciation that the features most requiring modernization were pre-heating of the cold feed water using waste heat from the exhaust, extra heating area in the firebox through the use of thermic syphons (flattened vertical ducts), a 24 per cent increase in the size of a more efficient but also more complex superheater, larger steam pipes for better steam flow, poppet rather than piston valves and slide valves, and a double chimney for more draught and reduced back pressure.

The improved 4500-class locomotive was so successful that the Paris-Orléans railway ordered the conversion of 31 3500-class locomotives in a similar fashion. During 1932, some 16 3500-class locomotives were also rebuilt to a similar but slightly less ambitious standard with piston heads carrying two rather than one valve to double the area of port opened in a set distance of movement.

In the same year, one of the remaining 4500-class locomotives without a superheating system was rebuilt into a 4-8-0 layout for investigation of the concept of creating an engine with one-third more adhesive weight. The change required a different boiler with a narrow firebox to fit between the rear driving wheels, but in other respects the rebuilding followed the Chapelon pattern even though the introduction of further refinement served to boost the available power. The prototype's successful conversion led to the rebuilding of 11 more engines to the same standard during 1934, and in 1940 some 25 more 4500-class locomotives were converted to a comparable standard boosted by the addition of a mechanical stoking system. By the 1960s the last of these Pacific-type locomotives were based at Calais to haul heavy boat trains arriving from the U.K. The locomotives were very effective in this role, being capable of hauling heavy trains up relatively steep gradients, but there could be no denial of the fact that the locomotives were heavy consumers of coal and were generally costlier to operate than simpler 2-8-2 locomotives of the 141R class that had been delivered from the U.S.A. after the end of World War II to boost the reconstruction of France.

The S3/6 class of Pacific-type 4-6-2 locomotives, which was introduced on the Royal Bavarian state railway in 1909, reflected both the geographic differences and design approaches between Bavaria and Prussia. Bavaria is considerably hillier or indeed more mountainous than Prussia, which is generally flat, and greater flair was revealed by Heinrich Leppla, the chief designer of Maffei, the primary manufacturer of Bavarian locomotives. This flair reached it apogee in a series of Pacific-type locomotives delivered for 23 years to the railways of Bavaria and Baden as well as to the German state railway that absorbed both of these operators in the 1920s.

Since 1895 the passenger locomotives of the Bavarian railway had been of the four-cylinder compound-expansion type, including two Atlantic-type locomotives bought during 1901 from Baldwin of the U.S.A. and, it appears, a major influence on Maffei as this company became the first European company to built locomotives of the bar frame type and also the first to cast the cylinders in substantial blocks including the smokebox saddle. All four of these cylinders powered the same axle, which in the Pacific type of locomotive was the central axle. The first S3/6-class locomotives were completed during 1908 for the railway of Baden, the first locomotives for the Bavarian railway following in the next year. Production of 23 such locomotives, with a driving wheel diameter of 6ft 1.6in (1.87m), had been completed by 1911, and these were followed by 18 locomotives with a driving wheel

The Caledonian, resplendent in the livery of the London, Midland & Scottish Railway (LMS), leaves Crewe for Carlisle.

diameter of 6ft 6.7in (2.00m), while another 78 locomotives were manufactured between 1913 and 1924 with the original size of driving wheel. This was far from the end of the story, for there were a number of other batches with more limited changes such as the addition of feed-water heaters, increased axle load, and higher steam pressure. The overall designation for the locomotives was the S3/6 class, which detailed an express locomotive (Schnellzuglokomotiv) with six axles of which three were powered.

During 1925 the newly created German state railway took delivery of the first of its standard Pacific-type locomotives. The axle load of these locomotives prevented their

employment on all but the most strongly constructed lines, so a class of smaller and therefore lighter Pacific-type locomotives was needed for the rest of the German rail network. As the new type was being designed and placed in production, though, the national railway operation had need of a Pacific-type locomotive with an axle load reduced from 20 to 18 tonnes. The obvious solution was further production of the excellent Maffei design, of which 40 were completed between 1927 and 1931. These locomotives were evident all over Germany until the advent of the definitive O3-class locomotive. The last of these classic locomotives was retired only in 1966.

In the first part of the 20th century the Belgian national railway built several classes of inside-cylinder locomotives bearing a strong conceptual relationship to the McIntosh locomotives of the Caledonian Railway. During 1904, however, there began a new era in the hands of J.B. Flamme, whose technical bent was aligned more with the French pattern of compound-expansion locomotive. Flamme borrowed such an engine for evaluation, which revealed that the French locomotive was clearly so much better than existing Belgian engines that an order was placed for 12 similar locomotives and then 57 of a compound-expansion 4-6-0 design. Flamme's next step was the manufacture of four 4-6-0 locomotives to a new design, and in these he was also to undertake an investigation of the superheating system in simple- and compound-expansion locomotives. This process permitted Flamme to opt for the simplicity and lower cost of the non-compound locomotive, although he appreciated that for the largest classes there were advantages in the use of four cylinders to give the improved level of balance revealed by the four-cylinder compound-expansion locomotives. The result was two classes of very large locomotives, namely a Pacific-type 4-6-2 for employment on express services and a 2-10-0 type for employment on freight services. The boilers of the two classes were basically similar except for a few small

The LMS Duchess of Hamilton, *a Duchess-class 4-6-2 locomotive at Bury, England. This class of locomotive was the most powerful ever to run in that country.*

differences in the size of their fireboxes, and the limiting factor for length was the upper weight figure for the 2-10-0 type. The boiler would have appeared short on any Pacific-type locomotive, but this fact was accentuated by a number of other features, and by the European concepts of the period the boiler was odd as it possessed a very large grate for the burning of low-grade coal. Walschaert valve gear was used for the valves of the two outside cylinders, and rocking shafts were employed to operate the valves of the two inside cylinders that powered the leading axle.

Some 28 of these locomotives were made between 1910 and 1928, 30 more following in 1929 and 1930 with a grate of smaller size and shortened rear end, changes that knocked 5 tonnes off the weight. Known as the 10 class under a later classification, these locomotives worked the express routes connecting Brussels with Liège and Luxembourg, and were highly effective. The Belgian national railway started a major refurbishment of its stock after World War I, and within the context of this programme fitted larger superheating systems, double

chimneys for improved draught, strengthened frames at the front, and a number of detail enhancements. The programme continued with the addition of smoke deflectors and feed-water heaters, and bogie tenders from German war-reparation engines replaced the original six-wheeled tenders. Spurred by the success of Chapelon's efforts in France, the Belgians launched another improvement effort in 1938 with features such as enlarged steam pipes, greater superheating area, and the replacement of the Legein double-chimney exhaust by the Kylchap pattern.

RIGHT: A Class A4
streamline 4-6-2, the
famous Pacific, which still
holds the world's speed
record for a steam
locomotive. It is probably
the favourite locomotive of
British rail enthusiasts.

RIGHT: A Class A4
streamline 4-6-2, the
famous Pacific, which still
holds the world's speed
record for a steam
locomotive. It is probably
the favourite locomotive of
British rail enthusiasts.

OPPOSITE: The Castle-
class 4-6-0 7001 Sir James
Milne near Westerleigh,
England with the
Cornishman.

These changes did little for the appearance of
the locomotives, but did produce the increase
in performance and tractive effort that had
been demanded. It was 1959 before the last
of these locomotives, in fact one of the first-
series machines, was finally retired.

Under the supervision of George Whale
and W.T. Bowen-Cooke, the London &
North Western Railway between 1903 and
1914 placed in service 336 new 4-4-0 and
4-6-0 express locomotives, all made at the
company's Crewe plant. Crewe built four
types of express locomotive in this time, and
one of these was truly outstanding. This was
the later of the two 4-4-0 types, the great

George V class of locomotives, of which the
first was delivered during 1910. The design
was in essence a much improved development
of the Precursor class of 1903 with more
modern features such as piston valves and a
superheating system. Some 90 George V-class
locomotives were built, to which must be
added a further 64 conversions from the
Precursor class as well as another 10 from the
Queen Mary class of 4-4-0 locomotives
without a superheating system. Despite their
limited 4-4-0 configuration, these
comparatively modest locomotives hauled
much of the prestige passenger traffic between
Euston and stations to the north. In the

George V class everything was consciously
made as simple as possible. The outer firebox
wrapper was of the round top rather than
more complicated Belpaire type, and while the
cylinders were of the inside type, the use of
the Joy-type valve gear, with rods and slides in
the same vertical plane as the connecting rods,
created a situation in which all the inside
motion was readily reached for lubrication and
maintenance.

The year 1923 saw the consolidation of
the multitude of British railway companies
into four large organizations, the George V-
class locomotives thereby coming into the
ownership of the London Midland & Scottish
Railway, a company controlled largely by ex-
Midland Railway men who had a low regard
for all locomotives originating outside this
company. It was hardly surprising, therefore,
that the retirement of these effective
locomotives started as early as 1935, ending
with the demise of the last unit in 1948.

The S class of massive 2-6-2 locomotives
introduced in 1911 for the Russian railway
network may have been the largest of all
steam locomotive classes as the construction
of such locomotives continued for 40 years
and its operation for more than 60 years. This
reflects the fact that, despite the ridicule in
which it was held by large numbers of the ill-
informed at the time and in later periods, the
imperial government of pre-revolutionary
Russia was in fact far ahead of its time in

Wood, not coal, fuels this Paraguayan locomotive.

locomotives was first manufactured during 1926 at the Kolomna factory near Moscow. Totalling about 2,400 locomotives over a 15-year period, this subclass may be regarded as the definitive standard, and the u in the designation stood for *usilennyi* (strengthened). The wheel base, boiler and cylinders were all enlarged but there was no increase in the boiler pressure over the modest figure inherited from the baseline S class, reflecting the fact that the cost-conscious Soviets felt that a higher boiler pressure would add unnecessary production and maintenance costs. After the end of World War II in 1945, manufacture was resumed at the Soromovo plant and continued until 1951, by which time some 3,750 S-class locomotives had been built. Variants comprised some Sv-class locomotives built in 1915 for the standard-gauge line from Warsaw south toward Vienna, and some Sum-class locomotives with a system for pre-heating the combustion air. Many of the S-class locomotives burned not coal but oil, a fuel that had been introduced in Russia as early as 1880 and soon became relatively common.

The Gresley A3-class 4472 Flying Scotsman at Carnforth. The Flying Scotsman *service was inaugurated on the first day of 1923, and covered the 404 miles (650km) between London and Edinburgh.*

matters of standardization, and this process continued after the Soviet Revolution of 1917 and the tumult of the years that followed. The S class of 2-6-2 locomotives was a standard design for general use among Russia's many independent railways. The S stood for the Soromovo works at Nizhnii Novgorod (later renamed Gorkiy) where the class was built,

and about 900 of these first-class locomotives were manufactured before the revolution. The design was an early example of what was in effect the standard definitive form of steam locomotive with two cylinders, Walschaert valve gear, a wide firebox, a superheating system, and compensated springing.

The Su class of larger, improved

Chapter Three
HEYDAY OF THE
STEAM LOCOMOTIVE

The Cornish Riviera Limited, *here photographed in 1953, originally began running in July 1904. It ran non-stop from London to Plymouth to reach Penzance in exactly 7 hours, though further reductions in time occurred later.*

As may be deduced from sections above, the French were among the first main exponents of steam locomotion to appreciate the theoretical advantages of compound expansion for steam engines used in express passenger work, and therefore exploited the notion with greater diligence and success than the steam locomotion engineers of any other country. Even so, doubt did sometimes creep into the minds of French engineers, and this led to the construction of groups of simple-expansion locomotives, but in overall terms the concept of compound expansion in general thrived and became ever more strong.

This tendency is well illustrated by the Pacific-type locomotives of the Paris, Lyons & Mediterranean railroad. Between 1890 and 1907 the railroad ordered just under 850 locomotives, of which no fewer than 835 were of the compound-expansion type, and in the period between 1905 and 1907 the manufacture of compound-expansion Atlantic type and 4-6-0 locomotives continued unabated. Then in 1907 there appeared the first European Pacific-type locomotive, and in 1909 the railroad produced two prototype locomotives with that type's 4-6-2 wheel layout, one with simple and the other with compound expansion. The availability of these two prototypes allowed the locomotive designers to test and, it was anticipated, reaffirm their belief in the superiority of compound expansion, but at the same time there was another reason for the manufacture of a locomotive of the simple-expansion type. It was known that compound expansion made its possible for a higher proportion of the steam's energy to be converted into work as it expanded, but also that the exploitation of the compound engine's full advantages required a high steam pressure, and that high pressure resulted in increased boiler maintenance requirement and therefore cost. In this second half of the 20th century's first decade, a novel attraction for engineers was the superheater, a system which offered the considerable improvement in the simple-expansion engine's thermal efficiency to the point at which it might once again be a contender for use in high-performance locomotives, which might thus be manufactured and maintained at the reduced overall costs resulting from the use of lower boiler pressures.

The availability of the two otherwise

No.7029 comes off the Royal Albert Bridge at Saltash on its return trip to Truro, celebrating the first steam train from Devon to Cornwall since 1964.

similar Pacific-type locomotives allowed the concept to be evaluated in real operational terms, for the compound-expansion engine used saturated steam whereas the simple-expansion engine had a superheating system. The compound-expansion locomotive had the standard de Glehn layout of cylinders, with the outside high-pressure cylinders located well back over the rear truck wheels, but the simple engine had an inline arrangement of its four cylinders, as in the railroad's existing Atlantic type and 4-6-0 locomotives. The

inline arrangement allowed a much more rigid structure than was possible with the de Glehn arrangement. In other respects the two prototypes were basically similar except for the fact that the compound-expansion engine worked at a higher steam pressure.

The two 231-class prototype locomotives were used for comparative trials during 1911, and an analysis of the results revealed that the superheated engine developed greater power but also burned 16 per cent less coal than the compound-expansion engine. The next step

In 1929, the prestigious train service operating from Victoria Station, London to Paris was given the name Golden Arrow, and the locomotives carried both the Union flag as well as the French tricolour.

During 1921 and 1931 the railway contracted for another 230 and 55 Pacific-type locomotives respectively for an overall total of 462. Within these orders, successive batches introduced gradual improvement, mainly to the proportions of the boiler and the exhaust arrangements, without any major alteration of the core layout. Improvements were gradually made, one of the last being based on the Chapelon package of upgrades to the steam passages and boiler proportions. The Chapelon package was evaluated in an engine which was rebuilt with a boiler having still higher pressure, and although a plan to retrofit this boiler was created, only 30 of the locomotives were fully modernized in this fashion, the last of them in 1948, after the Paris, Lyons & Mediterranean railway had been absorbed into the nationalized Société Nationale des Chemins de Fer. Another 284 locomotives were partially modernized.

These Pacific-type locomotives had prolonged and useful careers, but even in improved form they did not achieve the level of overall performance displayed by the Chapelon rebuilds of the Paris-Orléans railway's Pacific-type locomotives. From 1952 the locomotives were replaced in the main routes by electric locomotives, thereafter spending their declining years on other services. The retirement of the class began during the 1950s, but many of the boilers still

A 4-4-2 locomotive, built in 1926, heads a passenger train in Cairo, Egypt in 1945. Note that passenger carriages are painted white to reflect the heat.

could have been a combination of superheating and compound expansion, but during this period it was impossible to manufacture a superheated compound-expansion locomotive and remain within current weight restrictions. As a result, the Paris, Lyons & Mediterranean railway ordered 70 simple-expansion locomotives in 1911. In 1912, however, the design problems of the superheated type of compound-expansion engine had been overcome, and 20 such locomotives were manufactured to a pattern that differed from that of the prototype only in its inline arrangement of the

four cylinders. For some reason there was still a measure of uncertainty, however, and 20 more simple-expansion locomotives were then made before a 1913 evaluation of the two types of superheated design decided that the compound-expansion type offered improved performance as well as a 25 per cent reduction in coal consumption. With the issue of simple- and compound-expansion engines finally settled, the Paris, Lyons & Mediterranean railway ordered no further Pacific-type locomotives of the simple-expansion type, and existing engines of this type were gradually converted to compound-expansion operation.

RIGHT & OPPOSITE:
A Russian Class P36 heads
a passenger train. Russian
railways, particularly on
the Trans-Siberian route,
had strategic objectives in
mind other than the task of
carrying passengers.

had considerable life left in them allowing their use as replacements, and as a result the last of the 231C-class locomotives were not withdrawn until 1969.

Only on limited occasions were any of the world's great trains hauled solely by a tank engine, but a notable example of this breed was the *Southern Belle*, which was the Pullman express operating between London and Brighton. Specially associated with this train was a group of seven Baltic-class 4-6-4 locomotives, the most powerful engines ever operated by the London, Brighton & South Coast Railway. Express services between London and the south coast of England had previously been hauled mainly by 4-4-0, 4-4-2 and 4-4-2T locomotives. The new 4-6-4 locomotives were to a design that was to some degree a stretched version of the two 4-6-2T locomotives that had supplemented the other locomotives. Designed by Colonel L.B. Billinton, the class was created to provide locomotives able to haul the *Belle* and other fast trains such as the *City Limited* between London and Brighton in 45 to 50 minutes instead of 60 minutes. In fact, the 60-minute timing was never improved upon, even by the successor to the *Southern Belle*, the electric *Brighton Belle*, which replaced the steam train after 1933; but it has to be recognized that the addition of third-class Pullman carriages to the previous arrangement of just first-class carriages made

the train an increasingly heavy load.

Billinton followed the design and engineering conventions of the period except in the valve gear, which comprised outside Walschaert valve gear that operated inside piston valves between the frames via rocking levers. The primary reasons for this disposition were Billinton's desire for cylinders similar to those of the 4-6-2T locomotives and the need for a well tank under the boiler between the frames, an arrangement which would have been impossible had there been valve motion in the region. There was trouble with the first unit of the class, including a derailment as a result of the high centre of gravity combined with the sloshing of water in half-full tanks: the solution to this problem was found in making all but the lower 1ft 3in (0.381m) of the side tanks into dummies, an arrangement which lowered the locomotive's centre of gravity so successfully that speeds of up to 75mph (121km/h) were then quite often attained without problem.

The second unit of the class was delivered just before the outbreak of World War I in August 1914, and five further examples were made in 1921–22. Two more received names at that time, these being the *Stephenson* and the *Remembrance*, the latter being named for the railroad company's war dead and also giving its name to the entire class. The class's later units were never fitted with the feed-water heaters and steam-operated feed pumps

which, unusually in British practice, were fitted to the earlier ones for a time after their completion.

After the electrification of the line during 1933, the Southern Railway converted the 4-6-4 tank engines into 4-6-0 locomotives known as the N15X class, a guise in which they had a successful second career on the less exacting longer-distance services of the bigger system, lasting well after 1948 into the days after the nationalization of all the separate British railroad companies into the unified British Railways. The fact that this was deemed worth doing demonstrates clearly the high quality of these locomotives, whose last survivor was retired in July 1957.

If there was a single railroad that set the standards which the rest of the world's railroads generally hoped to emulate, it was the Pennsylvania Railroad. To this extent the Pennsylvania Railroad liked to consider itself the Standard Railroad of the World, and its magnificent K4 class of 4-6-2 steam locomotives, introduced in 1914 and soon the core of the railroad's operations until a time well after World War II, could be called the Standard Express Locomotive of the World. Following a number of other Pacific-type locomotives, the K4 class eventually totalled 425 engines completed in 14 years. In overall terms, the Pennsylvania Railroad was very conservative in the design and construction of its locomotives, preferring to progress by

An Australian W-class locomotive, now preserved. In the 1950s, this class of locomotive hauled the Broken Hill Express, *whose passenger services were eventually taken over by the* famous Indian-Pacific *service.*

limited steps before committing itself to a major manufacturing effort, and its adoption of the Pacific-type locomotive was prefaced by the evaluation of one K28-class prototype ordered in 1907 from the American Locomotive Company. By 1910 the Pennsylvania Railroad believed that it knew enough about the Pacific-type locomotive to embark on the construction of such locomotives to its own design, and soon 239 K2-class locomotives had been delivered.

Superheating was applied to these locomotives only in 1912.

In 1913 the Pennsylvania Railroad contracted with Baldwin of Philadelphia for 30 examples of the improved K3 class of 4-6-2 locomotives, whose main novelty was the installation of the earliest type of practical mechanical stoker. The Pennsylvania Railroad had used such a stoking system since 1905 and nearly 300 such systems were in use by 1914, only 64 of them on Pacific-type

locomotives. Later designs of stoker used a screw feed, but the initial type pushed the coal forward with a series of steam-powered paddles that were feathered on the return stroke to avoid levering the coal back again. The coal was fed into the firebox at grate level in a fashion unlike that which later became common, in which the stoker fed the coal onto a rear-mounted platform for further distribution by jets of steam. A different Alco prototype supplied in 1911 was the K29-class

South Australian Railway's 3ft 6-in (1.07-m) Class 400 4-8-2 and 2-8-4 No.407 leaving Port Pirie for Peterborough, originally Petersburg. Though here hauling freight, Garratt locomotives were used on the Broken Hill Express *passenger service for many years.*

locomotive, which was larger than the K28-class unit.

The K4-class prototype of the Pennsylvania Railroad's Pacific-type locomotives was completed during 1914. This prototype, owing much to the E6 class of Atlantic-type 4-4-2 locomotives, was considerably larger than the units of the K2 class and provided 36 per cent more tractive effort for a mere 9 per cent increase in axle loading. It is worth noting that the Pennsylvania Railroad differed from virtually every other North American railroad operator in its objective of self-sufficiency in the design

and manufacture of locomotives. A considerable asset in this capacity was the railroad's own locomotive testing facility at Altoona, and it was on this that the K4-class prototype was tested soon after its completion, the evaluation revealing that few changes were needed for the production version. Sustained operational use did indicate the need for a number of modifications and by 1923, with 200 or more K4-class locomotives completed, the hand-operated reversing gear of the earlier locomotives was replaced by a power-operated reversing arrangement. The earlier locomotives were

also adapted to the improved standard, and during the 1930s most of the K4-class locomotives were retrofitted with an automatic stoking system. Another major enhancement of the 1930s was the installation of a continuous cab-signalling system: a receiver picked up a coded current flowing in track circuits, and converted this into the relevant signal on a display in the cab.

Features typical of the Pennsylvania Railroad's conservative approach to technical improvements was evident in such things as the low ratio of evaporative heating surface to superheater size, and a boiler pressure only about 75 per cent of that typical in the locomotives of most other contemporary North American railroad operators. This should not be construed as any suggestion that these features were wrong, however, but only that they were different from the norm and geared to the particular operating environment of the Pennsylvania Railroad. Limited superheating and a comparatively low boiler pressure, for instance, reduced the amount of maintenance and repair that were necessary, and this suggested that the railroad had decided in overall terms that the benefits of lower maintenance and repair costs more than offset the associated higher fuel consumption.

Except for 75 units built by Baldwin, all the K4-class locomotives manufactured during 1924–28 were made at Altoona. There were a few specials among the K4-class fleet. For example, two locomotives with poppet valve gear, thermic syphons in the firebox, and improved draughting, offered a one-third increase in power, the K4sa subclass locomotives offered higher cylinder horsepower through the combination of the same type of firebox and exhaust improvements with enlarged piston valves, one locomotive was for a time fully streamlined, and a number of other locomotives were partly streamlined. Many types of tender were used, including a few which were so big they dwarfed the engine. Outside the railroad's area of electrification, the K4-class locomotives were responsible for hauling all of the Pennsylvania Railroad's express passenger services in the period before the introduction of the Duplex locomotives in the aftermath of World War II.

April 1922 was an important month in British railway history for it marked the arrival of the first of a new class of Pacific-type locomotives whose record can be matched by few others. Some 79 of what were known initially as the A1 class of 4-6-2 locomotives were made between 1921 and 1934 for service on the Great Northern Railway. The design by Nigel Gresley was based on the assumption that a large locomotive, with more than enough power for the task envisaged for it, might be costly to make but would be economical in operation over a long career as a result of its limited maintenance needs. The thinking behind the design also attested Gresley's knowledge that the locomotive should be kept as simple as possible, and that it was essential for the reciprocating forces to be balanced. This latter could be achieved by a minimum of three cylinders. Despite the

No.R707, a 4-6-4 express passenger locomotive, used to haul broad-gauge (5ft 3in/1.6m) passenger trains in Australia.

The last day of Australian Steam fortnight. No.3801 at Barry Road bridge en route from Melbourne to Albury, and thence to Sydney.

basic simplicity of these attractive locomotives, they suffered from poor design in their details. One of the worse aspects of the design was the valve gear, and this was modified during 1926 in a process that cost little to implement yet produced a major reduction in coal consumption. An appreciation of the need for the changes came in 1925, when a smaller 4-6-0 locomotive from the rival Great Western Railway was evaluated by the London & North Eastern Railway (an amalgamation of the Great Northern, Great Eastern, North Eastern, Great Central, North British and other smaller railway companies): this *Pendennis Castle* achieved everything that the A1-class locomotive could manage but with a 10 per cent lower fuel consumption.

The LNER's engineers then examined another Castle-class locomotive's valve gear and then improved the valve gear of the A1 class to the extent that its coal consumption was reduced by 20 per cent by comparison with its previous figure. The reduction in coal consumption was sufficient for a locomotive of the A1 class to haul an express passenger train from London to Newcastle without the engine change that had previously been needed. A boiler intended for operation at higher pressure was then introduced: the change increased the locomotive's weight and axle loading, but the overall result was worth the extra cost and weight. The locomotives fitted with these boilers were designated as

the A3 class of what was sometimes known as Super-Pacific engines. From 1928 these locomotives were able to undertake the longest non-stop journey in the world, namely the 395miles (636km) between London and Edinburgh, with the aid of special corridor tenders so that crews could be changed en route. In 1935 one of the locomotives made a high-speed run from London to Newcastle to test the way for the planned *Silver Jubilee* express with a 240-minute schedule, and covered the distance of 270 miles (435km) in 3 hours 50 minutes at an average speed of 69.9mph (112.5km/h). A streamlined version of the A1 class entered service to operate the new high-speed service, and the arrival of the streamlined locomotives allowed the older 4-6-2 locomotives to be displaced from their prime position on the East Coast main line. The demands of rail transport in World War II resulted in the operation of 24-coach trains on the East Coast main line, and the excellent performance of the A3- and surviving A1-class locomotives was an eloquent testimony to the brilliance of their concept but also, as a result of poorer maintenance, of their poor detail design. After the war efforts were made to remedy the worst of the poor design features, but progress was slowed by resistance from the design office, which felt that the locomotives were essentially right. The classes were widely used to 1965, and the last was retired only in 1965.

Another important type of locomotive, and one that completed more than 30 years of effective service in first-line express work, was the Royal Scot class of the London Midland & Scottish Railway. The type was introduced in 1927, but mid-way through their lives the locomotives were subjected to a rebuilding that left little of the original, a fact which perhaps detracts somewhat from their achievement. In the mid-1920s what was then the new LMS Railway realized that it lacked a locomotive able to haul the railway's most important service, the *Scottish Express* from London to Edinburgh and Glasgow, and soon named as the *Royal Scot*. As an expedient, a combination of one 4-6-0 and one 4-4-0 locomotive, lately of the London & North-Western Railway, hauled the service from London as far as Carnforth, where two of the LMS Railway's own 4-4-0 locomotives took over for the haul across the Lowlands of Scotland to Edinburgh and thence Glasgow.

After borrowing from the GWR a Castle-class 4-6-0 locomotive that proved eminently suitable and then considering the purchase of 25 similar units for service from the summer of 1927, the LMS Railway contracted in February 1927 with the North British Locomotive Company of Glasgow for the design and construction of 50 4-6-0 express locomotives. The late signature of the contract meant that the first of the new Royal Scot-class locomotives was not ready for

A Chai He forestry railway's 0-8-0, transporting a log train towards a river bridge in China.

service in the summer of that year as originally hoped, but entered service in November 1927.

The design was based on the use of three cylinders, each with its own set of Walschaert valve gear and a tubular barrel boiler with a Belpaire firebox as big as the loading gauge would allow. The Royal Scot class was not innovative in any technical sense, but made excellent use of all that was best in current locomotive technology. As a result the locomotives were able to undertake the role demanded of them without any problem: of the 50 units, half were allocated the name of British regiments and the other half the names of earlier locomotives now out of service, although the latter were later given regimental names.

Inevitably, there were a few teething problems to be overcome as the locomotives entered service: the piston valves leaked as they became worn, increasing steam consumption by almost 50 per cent; and the driver's forward field of vision was often obscured by smoke in a fashion that led to one accident and was remedied by the introduction of smoke deflectors. In 1930 the original units were supplemented by 20 more locomotives made by the previous Midland Railway works at Derby, and this batch of engines included a few non-regimental names such as *The Royal Air Force*, *The Girl Guide* and *The Boy Scout*.

RIGHT, BELOW &
OPPOSITE: The
production of closely-related
passenger and freight
locomotives, as shown here,
was favoured by Russian
authorities, though a large
number of steam
locomotives were imported
from Germany.

In the late 1920s and early 1930s there was considerable experimentation into ways of enhancing the locomotive's thermal efficiency through an increase in the pressure and thus the temperature of the steam. As a result the LMS Railway ordered another Royal Scot-class locomotive to a pattern that differed from that of the other 70 units in its Schmidt-pattern boiler which generated steam at a higher pressure and temperature to power a separate system generating steam at a lower pressure and temperature. These two systems fed their steam to one high-pressure and two low-pressure compound cylinders, which were conventionally arranged except that the feed to the two low-pressure cylinders was supplemented by steam from yet another compartment in the now increasingly complex steam-generation arrangement. The locomotive was named *Fury*, and after the death of one man and serious injury to another in a steam-breach accident, the locomotive was discarded.

During 1933 a new chief designer had reached the LMS Railway in the form of William Stanier, latterly of the GWR that was at the time considered to be the British leader in the design and operation of steam locomotives. Stanier introduced four improvements that impinged on the further history of the Royal Scot-class locomotives: the belated solution of axlebox troubles by a new design of bearing, the introduction of a

of the class could cope with all British express trains without any difficulty and also with greater fuel economy that their primary rivals, the larger 4-6-2 locomotives. The 70 locomotives of the Royal Scot class disappeared from service quickly and completely as British Railways started to introduce diesel locomotives: the first unit to be taken out of service was *The Welch Regiment* in October 1962 and the last was the *Scots Guardsman* which was retired and set aside for preservation as one of the three Royal Scot-class locomotives to have survived.

A near contemporary of the Royal Scot class but massing more than twice as much, the Class A 4-8-4 locomotive of the Northern Pacific Railroad entered service in the U.S.A. earlier in the same year. Although it had taken all but a century for the steam locomotive to evolve from the 0-2-2 layout to the 4-8-4 configuration, the probable efficacy of the configuration had begun to be appreciated in the U.S.A. during the mid-1920s and as a result appeared in service with several railways at much the same time. The first, by a small margin, was the Northern Pacific Railroad, a fact signalled by the alternative naming of the configuration as the Northern type even though the Canadian National Railway and the Delaware, Lackawanna & Western Railroad, which also introduced the 4-8-4 layout in 1927, respectively tried to gain acceptance of the type names Confederation

new and larger type of tender, the rebuilding of the *Fury* as the *British Legion* with a tapered-barrel boiler that paved the way for the introduction of boilers of improved pattern, and the design of a new class of 4-6-2 locomotive to replace the Royal Scot from premier services. This last was needed urgently, for more than 10 years of hard work had affected the Royal Scot-class locomotives to a marked degree. It was therefore decided that instead of being reboilered along the original pattern with a parallel boiler, the Royal Scot-class locomotives would be fitted with the newer type of tapered-barrel boiler for commonality with Stanier's other

locomotives. Other extensive changes were incorporated into the rebuild, and the first revitalized locomotive re-entered service in 1942 at the start of a programme that lasted to 1955. The rebuilt locomotives were transformed: the new engines were better able to sustain the wear and tear of high-speed running, heavy loads and lack of adequate maintenance during World War II and its aftermath.

In the trials which took place in 1948, shortly after the nationalization of the U.K.'s main-line railways, the locomotives of the Royal Scot class performed notably well. It also became clear that the 4-6-0 locomotives

RIGHT: A Russian Su-class 2-6-2 locomotive, of which more than 2,000 were built in 15 years. The 'S' stood for the Soromovo works where the class was built, and the 'u' for usilennyi, which means 'strengthened'.

BELOW: The Russian S class was a standard-design locomotive used by many independent railways before the Russian Revolution.

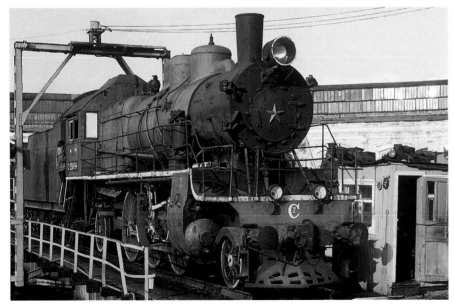

and Pocono respectively. Eventually, more than 40 operators in North America had 4-8-4 locomotives.

The origin of the 4-8-4 layout can be found in the lack of balance between theoretical tractive effort and grate area in the preceding 4-8-2 locomotives. This presented a major problem for the Northern Pacific Railroad as the coal from its local (and therefore cheapest and most readily accessible) source yielded a comparatively larger volume of ash: this meant that the railroad's locomotives needed a large firebox and a four- rather two-wheel rear truck. The firebox

introduced on the railroad's 4-8-4 Class A locomotives was larger than that of any other 4-8-4-class unit, but the operator found the Class A locomotive so successful that it adhered to the same basic pattern for all its passenger locomotives as long as it operated steam engines: the railroad ordered its last steam locomotives in 1943, and the intervening Class A-2, Class A-3, Class A-4 and Class A-5 unit were to patterns that were in essence improved subvariants of the Class A design.

The original 12 Class A locomotives were made by the American Locomotive Company, and these units were followed by a one-off ordered by the Timken Roller Bearing Company for operation by the Northern Pacific Railroad for successful validation of the advantages claimed for the company's roller bearings. All the other Class A locomotives were completed by Baldwin, which thus delivered 10 Class A-2 units in 1934, eight Class A-3 units in 1938, eight Class A-4 units in 1941 and 10 Class A-5 units in 1943.

That the 4-8-4 layout did not immediately sweep away its major rivals right across the U.S.A. is supported by the introduction during 1927 of the Class J type of 4-6-4 by the New York Central Railroad. In 1926 the New York Central Railroad completed its last Pacific-type locomotive, a Class K5b unit, and under the supervision of Paul W. Kiefer started to plan a larger locomotive to offer

A striking example of Russian steam power.

locomotive of very distinct and striking appearance with greater tractive power and, as a result of the 4-6-4 layout, a lower axle weight.

Once this first locomotive had proved its capabilities, the New York Central Railroad placed additional orders for locomotives to be used by itself (145 Class J1a to Class J1e units) and three subsidiary railways (80 units) including the Boston & Albany Railroad whose 30 locomotives were the units of the Class J2a, Class J2b and Class J2c types with minor differences. From the beginning of their careers, the Class J locomotives acquired an excellent reputation for their ability to haul heavy trains at high speed: a typical load was 18 cars weighing 1,270 tonnes at a speed of 55mph (88km/h) on the generally level sections.

The last Class J1 and Class J2 locomotives were completed in 1932, and there followed an interval as improvements to the basic design were carefully considered and evaluated. Thus it was 1937 before the 50 locomotives of the Class J3 type were ordered, these incorporating a number of improvements including a combustion chamber in the firebox, a tapered-boiler barrel to give a greater diameter at the front of the firebox for a useful increase in steam pressure, cylinders of reduced diameter but longer stroke, and disc driving wheels. The last 10 of these locomotives were completed to a

sufficient power for the railway's increasingly heavy trains. As fixed by Kiefer, the primary needs in the new type were greater starting tractive effort, more cylinder power at higher speeds, and better distribution of weight and balance to reduce the locomotive's impact on the track. Success in meeting these objectives clearly required a larger firebox and, in order to reduce the axle loading, a four-wheeled truck under the cab to create a 4-6-4 configuration. Despite the fact that the Lima Locomotive Works had exercised a considerable influence in the creation of the basic design, the New York Central Railroad

contracted with the American Locomotive Company for the first locomotives, though Lima later built 10 units of what later became known as the Hudson type.

The first Class J1a unit was delivered in February 1927 as the first 4-6-4 locomotive to be completed in the U.S.A. even though similar engines were being built by Alco for other operators. By comparison with the Class K5b locomotive, the Class J1a unit had a larger grate and a boiler of increased diameter and greater pressure in combination with cylinders and driving wheels that were unaltered in diameter. The net effect was a

RIGHT: Another Russian example.

RIGHT: The Rimatuka Incline near Wellington on the North Island of New Zealand where several engines were interspersed along the train to climb the steep slope using the Fell system of braking.

streamlined standard with an outer casing to reduce drag.

The Class J3 locomotives soon revealed themselves to be superior to the Class J1 units in terms of power and efficiency, as revealed by the ability of such a locomotive to haul a 1,130-tonne train over the 150 miles (241km) between Albany and Syracuse at a speed of 59mph (95km/h). The New York Central Railroad's most prestigious service at this time was the *20th Century Limited* linking New York and Chicago. The introduction of the Class J1e locomotive allowed the scheduled time of 20 hours to be trimmed to 18 hours during 1932, falling to 16 hours during 1938 after the introduction of the Class J3 locomotive.

The Class J locomotives operated by the New York Central Railroad's subsidiaries were later added to the main operator's fleet, giving the New York Central Railroad 275 Class J locomotives. After the end of World War II in 1945, the Class J locomotives were replaced on the railway's premier services by Niagara-class 4-8-4 locomotives, but as only 25 of these were produced there was still much for the Class J units to do until they were replaced by diesel-engined locomotives in the period between 1953 and 1956.

As noted above, the end of World War I had seen the dispersal of many Prussian locomotives, most especially the 4-6-0 units of the P8 class, as part of Germany's reparations

An early Canadian Northern Railway freight train passing a typical grain elevator.

The Soviet P36 class was originally designed for passenger service but was subsequently used for hauling heavy freight.

to members of the victorious Allied powers. Germany started a programme to make good these losses to its own railroad system, and in 1919 began work on a 2-8-2 locomotive for secondary passenger traffic in Germany's hillier regions. Work on the P10 class of 2-8-2 locomotives was delayed by a number of post-war difficulties, and although it had been designed more specifically for service on the Prussian railroad network, the German state railway had come into existence by the time the first locomotive was completed by Borsig during 1922. The design drew on Prussian

locomotive experience in the previous quarter of a century, but the single class that had the highest influence on the design was the G12 class of 2-10-0 locomotives built in 1917 to meet the urgent need for a powerful goods engine for lines of medium axle load. To speed the design process, the G12-class locomotive was based on a Henschel design for the Turkish railroad, and it introduced some novel features to a Prussian design, particularly bar frames and a Belpaire firebox with a trapezoidal grate above the driving wheels. These G12-class design features were

translated into the P10-class locomotive, which also had three cylinders. The introduction of larger driving wheels meant that there was not enough clearance for the firebox above the driving wheels, so the grate was made in three sections: the parallel front part was located between the rear driving wheels, the intermediate part was outwardly tapered, and the rear part was parallel and the same in width as the widest portion of the intermediate part. The arrangement set the firebox farther forward, and thus gave a better weight distribution with more weight on the driving wheels, but the shape was complex and resulted in higher maintenance costs, and was not repeated.

The introduction of a nationwide and nationalized German railway system in 1922 led to the redesignation of the P10 class as the 39 class, of which some 260 examples were completed between 1922 and 1927. Though notionally engines for use on secondary passenger services, the P10-class locomotives were in fact true mixed-traffic engines, and shared their time between passenger and freight work until the disappearance of the last unit during 1967. After World War II the survivors of the class were split between East Germany and West Germany, 85 of the East German engines being rebuilt with new boilers, round-topped fireboxes and wide grates. In overall terms, the P10 class should be regarded as the apogee of Prussian steam locomotive design, but it was also important as marking the transition to the German state standard locomotives, experience with the P10 class being available before the design of the standard locomotives was finally settled upon.

During 1922 a Central Locomotive Design Section was established under Dr. R.P. Wagner, and this section's first task was the creation of standard locomotives based on Prussian practice but taking into account the need for the new locomotives that would be required to operate in all parts of Germany, and would therefore need the ability to run capably on low-grade coal and also to climb gradients steeper than those typical of Prussia. These two factors demanded larger grates and, in locomotives with trailing carrying wheels, a clear space under the firebox for the entry of air and the removal of ashes.

The first of the classes were a pair of Pacific types designated as the 01 and 02 classes, which were basically similar in concept except for the fact that the locomotives of the 01 and 02 classes were of the two-cylinder simple-expansion and four-cylinder compound-expansion types respectively. Ten examples of each class were initially completed for trials in typical regions of Germany, resulting in the decision to standardize the 01 class as this was cheaper to build and maintain even though the fuel consumption of the 02 class was less. The 01 class was basically simple in concept but fairly complex in detail,

London & North Eastern Railway Garratt U1-class locomotive No.2395. Articulated locomotives such as the Garratt got round the problems caused by very long-boilered locomotives on curves.

Norfolk & Western Y6B Mallet No.2142 (2-8-8-2) on an eastbound freight-train taking water at Relspring, Virginia.

especially as it included auxiliary equipment including a feed-water heater with its heat exchanger in the smokebox ahead of the chimney. The detail design of the 01-class locomotive was the work of the Borsig company of Berlin, and manufacture was initially entrusted to Borsig and AEG. The first such locomotives were finished in 1926, and by 1938 some 231 new engines had been produced, a figure to which must be added the 10 02-class units converted to 01-class standard. Practical experience with the first engines suggested that later engines

have larger-diameter cylinders, boiler tubes lengthened in a fashion made possible by the shortening of the smokebox and, as a final step, the copper firebox replaced by a steel unit. Other changes included better brakes and larger truck wheels, allowing an increase in the maximum speed from 75mph (120km/h) to 81mph (130km/h).

In the meantime, during 1930, a slightly scaled-down version of the 01 class, designated as the 03 class, had been introduced for lines with a lower axle weight limit, and 298 of these smaller

engines were built up to 1937.

Up to 1937 the speed limit over most of Germany was 62mph (100km/h), but was then raised to 75mph (120km/h). Thus it was only from 1937 that the locomotives of the 01 and 03 classes could reveal their real capabilities. The speed limit was further increased in 1939, and when additional locomotives were manufactured a maximum speed of 93mph (150km/h) was demanded. In the light of the German railroad's experience with the 05 class of 4-6-4 locomotives, the new engines were fully streamlined and given a three-cylinder motive system. These new units were designated as 01-10 and 03-10 class locomotives, of which 55 and 60 examples respectively were completed between 1939 and 1941. These were the last new series-built express steam locomotives built in Germany. Soon after the end of World War II, 70 and 171 examples of the 01 classes were in service in East Germany and West Germany respectively. Of these, 35 East German and 55 West German engines were rebuilt. The last West German locomotives of this family were retired during 1973, but several of the East German units were operated into the first part of the 1980s, returned to regular service in an effort to overcome East Germany's shortage of oil. These were the last express steam locomotives in Europe.

The magnificent Beyer-Garratt locomotive, favourite for hauling freight in many parts of the world, particularly in Africa and Australia.

Chapter Four
SWANSONG AND
PRESERVED STEAM

*The basic Beyer-Garratt
locomotive consists of two
separate locomotive units
which share a large
common boiler.*

Although the rail transport of freight rather than passengers had been the driving force behind the creation of the first railways, it was the *Royal George* locomotive for the Stockton & Darlington Railway that signalled a new start in the development of the steam locomotive. Designed by Timothy Hackworth in 1827, the *Royal George* was the first 0-6-0 unit built for the mixed-traffic role,

and as such the engine inaugurated the emergence of an entirely new type of locomotive that would, early in the 20th century, then evolve into the definitive type of heavy freight locomotive.

During the main period of the Victorian age there were two main types of locomotive, one dedicated to the hauling of passenger and the other optimized for the hauling of freight

trains. In the earlier part of the railroad age, the passenger locomotive was generally of the 0-4-2 or 2-4-0 layout, while the freight locomotive or, as it was often called at the time, the baggage locomotive was generally a tank or tender engine of the 0-6-0 layout. By the 1880s most British and an increasing number of European railway and railroad companies were using larger 0-6-0 freight locomotives and indeed undertaking their first experiments with 0-8-0 locomotives for the hauling of freight trains. The longer trains of the U.S.A. were the norm, so locomotive designers created larger and heavier engines of the 2-6-0 and 2-8-0 layout for the hauling of heavy freight trains. These locomotives, of the bar-frame construction favoured by the Americans, were well suited to the comparatively rough country and poor track of the early U.S. railroads, and were also manufactured in significant numbers for export to South America, Australia and New Zealand, all of them regions in which conditions similar to those of the U.S.A. prevailed and therefore suggested the adoption of the American rather than

No.5505 of the East African Railway, built by Beyer-Peacock in 1945 for the Tanganyika Railway.

the European solution to their railroad requirements.

The progression of the 19th century saw a steady but nonetheless remarkable increase in the weight and diversity of the goods carried by freight trains. As a result, by the beginning of the 20th century many European and North American railroads were beginning to consider more effective means of hauling their heavy freight trains, which now had to move not only ever increasing quantities of freight items but also considerably heavier bulk loads such as coal and the raw materials required to feed the burgeoning industry. It was obvious that current freight-optimized locomotives were inadequate for the task of hauling the longer and heavier trains now demanded. In Europe, this led to the production of significantly heavier freight-hauling and switching locomotives characterized by their 0-8-0, 0-10-0 and 2-10-0 layouts.

GMA Garratt No.4165 shunts in factory sidings at Pietermaritzburg, South Africa. These locomotives were in demand for hauling freight in Africa.

Most notably in Germany and Austria, a number of standard locomotive classes were created for the task. A major figure in this process was an Austro-Hungarian citizen, Karl Gölsdorf. Credited with 45 locomotive designs, Gölsdorf created several classes of successful 2-8-0 and 2-10-0 heavy freight locomotives that were operated within the Austro-Hungarian empire and also exported in numbers to other countries in Europe,

including as a particularly notable example, Greece, whose state railroad system operated freight services using a large fleet of 2-8-0 and 2-10-0 locomotives imported from Austria-Hungary.

In Germany, the Royal Prussian state railroad system designed a number of standard classes of heavy freight locomotives based on the extensive use of common but well proven parts for maximum economy of manufacture

and maintenance in combination with the highest possibility level of reliability. These locomotives included the units of the G8 0-8-0, G10 0-10-0 and 44 classes, which were still in limited production when the various German railways were combined and nationalized into the German state railway during 1922. Like their Austro-Hungarian cousins, these German standard designs were also exported in large numbers to other

European railroad organizations, including those of Bulgaria, Poland, Romania and Turkey that all had strong economic and/or strategic ties with Germany.

At first lacking significant national industrial and engineering capability, Russia started by importing locomotives and other equipment mainly from Germany and the U.K., to provide an initial capability from the 1830s. These imported engines also offered Russian locomotive designers the core knowledge that allowed them to start producing effective Russian locomotive designs, albeit with a strong British or

German influence clearly evident at the beginning and then supplemented by American thinking. Factories for the manufacture of all types of railway equipment were soon established and started to make locomotives that were better suited than imported engines to the particular geographic and climatic conditions in which the Russian railroads operated. American influence grew as the Russian railroad system expanded from the core region of western Russia into the less civilized outer reaches of the empire, where conditions more closely approximated those of the U.S.A. as its railroads expanded across

the North American continent. The need to construct large numbers of standard passenger and freight locomotives, together with the ever increasing length and weight of trains required for the movement of larger numbers of passengers and greater quantities of freight, heralded the production of the O class of standard 0-8-0 locomotives. This locomotive, designed in the Tsarist period, was so successful that, with only minor modifications, it was built by Russian locomotive manufacturing plants right into the first two decades of the 20th century.

The development of an indigenous

A British Black 8 2-8-0 with a mixed freight near Chippenham, Wiltshire, England.

The Auckland-Wellington express headed by a K-class 4-8-4 locomotive No.905 between Taupiri and Ngaruawahia in Waikato district. 7 March 1952.

Russian locomotive design and manufacturing capability did not mean that the various private and state-owned railways relied exclusively on locomotives of Russian origin. Right up to the revolution of November 1917, which resulted in the establishment of the U.S.S.R. under a communist leadership with wholly different political, economic and social agendas, Russian railways were at various times buying and receiving large numbers of 0-8-0, 0-10-0 and, shortly before the outbreak of World War I in 1910, 2-10-0 steam locomotives from Germany and the U.S.A. By the 1920s the Soviet government had designed and manufactured several standard classes of locomotive for heavy freight use. These included the E and FD classes of 0-10-0 and 2-10-2 locomotives, to supplement the American-built Baldwin and Alco 2-10-0 locomotives supplied to Russia during World War I. The relationship of the

The 125th anniversary Victorian Government Railways 4-6-0.

The Orient Express *service, the epitome of luxurious and exotic travel, was launched (though not by that name) in 1883.*

FD class with other Soviet locomotives of the period reveals how the U.S.S.R. was generally happy, after finding an adequate industrial solution to a perceived economic need, to maintain the solution in production and service without consideration of any major concept of modernization: if a locomotive was technically successful in meeting state needs and was cheap both to build and to operate, it was kept in production and service in its original form and also in any variants that could readily be derived from it. Thus, when by 1930 it had created the very effective S class of passenger locomotives, of which some 3,000 were built for long-term service without any consumer pressure for radical improvement, the Soviet authorities could take their time in assessing the longer-term needs of a growing requirement for passenger transport, which up to this time had been secondary in Soviet thinking to the demands for the freight transport on which the much-desired industrialization of the Soviet state was heavily dependent. It was now appreciated that higher speeds and more comfortable (thus weightier) trains would eventually be needed.

The first prototype of a new generation of locomotives appeared during 1932 as what was really little more than an expansion of the S class of 2-6-2 locomotive into a 2-8-4 layout with an extra coupled axle for more tractive effort, and also an additional carrying

Garratt 742 No.19, en route to Bulawayo, Zimbabwe.

axle at the rear to allow the incorporation of a larger firebox so that the engine could generate more power for the use of the improved motive system. The design was designated as the IS class, and 640 such locomotives were manufactured in the period between 1934 and the time of the German invasion of the U.S.S.R. in 1941. The type has disappeared from service in its original passenger train version, but a derived freight version (with the same boiler, cab, cylinders, tender and other parts) is the FD class of 2-10-2 locomotives, of which substantial numbers were in use throughout southern China after being adapted to standard gauge from the Russian 5ft 0in (1.524m) gauge.

The production of closely related passenger and freight locomotives was of course typical of the Soviet authorities' approach, both financially sensible and technically logical, toward the needs of the state railroad system. To this extent, therefore, the Soviet regime differed only marginally from the Tsarist system it replaced. Also typical of the Soviet system, however, was the manufacture in 1937 and 1938 of the first three of a planned total of 10 streamlined 4-6-4 locomotives to haul the high-speed *Red Arrow* express between Moscow and Leningrad, a journey of slightly more than 400 miles (644km) on which an average speed of 40.5 to 50mph (65 to 80km/h) was planned. The initial pair of locomotives each had driving wheels with a diameter of 6ft 6.75in (2.00m) but the third unit had driving wheels with a diameter of 7ft 2.5in (2.19m). All three of the locomotives were based in design and mechanical detail on the FD class, with which they shared the boilers, cylinders and much else. The German invasion prevented the construction of the last seven of the locomotives, but early services had

A Union Pacific 4-6-6-4 Challenger-class locomotive No.3964 taking on coal. It originated from 1942.

revealed the class to provide excellent performance including a maximum speed of 106mph (170km/h).

The steadily growing weight and length of passenger and freight trains during the second half of the 19th century had made it clear by the beginning of the 20th century, at least to the larger and more far-sighted railroad organizations, that the continued success of steam-powered railway services in all but the flattest and smallest countries demanded the introduction of either larger and more powerful locomotives or of banking, or helper, locomotives to ease heavy trains over hilly country. Obviously the former was the

simpler solution, but it also meant that much of the new locomotives' power would be unnecessary for the more level and less demanding majority of any railway network, while the latter required the adoption of new locomotives that could be reserved for use on only the steeper gradients where the standard main-line locomotives needed their assistance. For some time the larger railway companies had used ordinary 4-4-0 and 0-6-0 locomotives for this purpose and found the concept adequate. By the late 1880s, though, it was clear that the demands of banking what had become considerably longer and heavier trains, with further increases inevitable,

required more powerful (and therefore larger) banking locomotives.

In the first part of the 20th century the British-run railways of India faced problems similar to those typical of North America. The need to bank trains over steeper gradients required the design and manufacture of a class of heavy tank locomotive built to the 0-8-4T arrangement. These locomotives, along with some 2-8-4T engines, were used on the Ghat Incline of the Great Indian Peninsula Railway. South African Railways were quick to appreciate the importance of powerful banking locomotives and, shortly before World War I, ordered a batch of Mallet-type locomotives from North British of Glasgow. These machines were used on heavy freight and banking duties until the early 1950s, when they were withdrawn. New Zealand Railways also needed a solution to the difficulty of moving large passenger and freight trains over difficult terrain. Rather than adopt the banking engine solution, however, the New Zealanders decided to approach the problem from a different angle and opted for the construction of an incline railroad using the Fell system of braking, which required the manufacture of specially designed 0-4-2 tank locomotives. The Fell braking system worked from a central rail that retarded the locomotive and train working on railway lines with a steep gradient: this frequently required the use of several

The American Big Boy, perhaps the definitive class of locomotive for heavy freight haulage.

RIGHT: A double-headed steam train hauls mixed freight on the Jingpeng line. China has one of the most elaborate and specialized railroad systems in the world.

OPPOSITE: A K36 2-8-2 leaves Durango, Colorado.

locomotives working together, depending on the weight of the train being banked.

Probably the first North American railroad to appreciate the problem of banking locomotives was the Baltimore & Ohio Railroad, which in 1904 had realized the right solution to the problem. Thus the Baltimore & Ohio Railroad built the first American example of the banking locomotive type developed by Anatole Mallet with two sets of coupled wheels: the leading set was pivoted to become a motor bogie or truck, in the process turning the Mallet locomotive into a semi-articulated unit. The Baltimore & Ohio

Railroad's Mallet-type locomotive, nicknamed *Old Maud*, was used for experiments in the banking of heavy trains over long and twisting gradients that otherwise required the use of multiple-heading of locomotives. The *Old Maud* proved very useful, and most of the larger railroad operators in North America then acquired Mallet locomotives of the same basic type or alternatively more conventional 2-8-0 or 2-10-0 locomotives to bank heavy trains up steeper gradients.

In the U.K. the Midland Railway constructed a 0-10-0 tender locomotive nicknamed *Big Emma* or sometimes *Big*

Bertha. Built in 1919, this locomotive was used on the Lickey Incline at Bromsgrove near Birmingham in the Midlands, where it remained in successful service up to 1956, when it was replaced by a 9F-class 2-10-0 locomotive. At much the same time, for the Great Central Railway, John G. Robinson designed some 0-8-4 tank engines for the related task of heavy hump shunting in goods yards. These locomotives survived into the later part of the 1940s, in the process lasting long enough to be taken into the stock of privately owned locomotives inherited by the nationalized British Railways organization. In

1925, the London & North Eastern Railway ordered a Beyer-Garratt locomotive for service on the Worsborough Incline near Barnsley in Yorkshire. This 2-8-8-2 locomotive remained in service until the line was electrified in 1955, after which it was tried on the Lickey Incline in company with *Big Bertha* and withdrawn only in 1956. In 1921 the London & South Western Railway ordered three examples of a 4-8-0 tank locomotive designed by Robert Urie, and these engines were employed at the new marshalling yard at Feltham on the edge of London to hump-shunt freight wagons into formation. All three of the locomotives were withdrawn from service in 1962.

The Mallet type of semi-articulated locomotive had first appeared in the alpine regions of Europe during 1889, but found only a modest level of acceptance. As can be deduced from the above, however, the Americans were more chary even of evaluating the type and thus it was 1904 before the Baltimore & Ohio Railroad came to believe that the type would also be useful for the hauling of very heavy coal trains and designed a huge double 0-6-0 locomotive. This engine was immediately a great success, and the U.S. railroads soon adopted the Mallet type of locomotive in increasing numbers as bankers and prime movers for heavy freight trains. The Mallet type of locomotive was not characterized by any high level of

RIGHT: A Northern
Pacific passenger train
leaving Desmet, Montana.
12 November 1939.

OPPOSITE: A Chinese
coal train on the Nanking
bridge. Coal and iron ore
are hauled extensively by
rail in China.

performance, in terms of either speed or
acceleration, but was very powerful indeed
and also notably easy on the road. Thus the
Mallet type of locomotive, which had started
as a small double-0-4-0 tank engine, then
matured in the U.S.A. as a heavy hauler of
increasing size and power. The finest example
was perhaps the *Matt H. Shay* of the Erie
Railroad before World War I, which had two
sets of coupled wheels, in each case
comprising four axles, and a third essentially
identical set under the tender to provide an
overall 2-8-8-8-2 layout for what became
known as the Triplex configuration. There
was nothing new in the concept of the steam-
powered tender, which had been
manufactured and used by both the Ouest
railroad in France and the Great Northern
Railway in the U.K. during the middle part of
the previous century, in both cases for
additional traction during difficult moments
such as starting and continued motion up
steep gradients. The concept of the powered
tender had a major problem, however, in all
of its forms, namely the relative shortage of
steam for all the cylinders that had to be
operated.

The type of long locomotive introduced
to provide greater tractive effort in the
particular low-performance environment
typical of freight operations had a long boiler,
and this presented difficulties on railway tracks
with all but the gentlest of curves. As a result

Two Chinese QJ-class locomotives haul freight in the Gobi desert of inner Mongolia. 'QJ' stands for Qing Jing or 'March Forward'.

Garratt locomotive consisted of two distinct motor units supporting between them, by means of pivots and bearings, the girder frame that carried the proportionally large boiler. Garratt's original idea had been that this arrangement would allow the creation of a large, powerful, yet flexible passenger locomotive in which the dimensions of the boiler would not be limited by the height of the large-diameter driving wheels, as was the case with more conventional steam locomotives. Such a passenger locomotive, with a 2-4-0+0-4-2 wheel arrangement, was in fact manufactured for the São Paulo Railway of Brazil during 1915, but the very first of the type were a few small double 0-4-0 locomotives for very narrow gauges, typified by the singular 2ft 0in (0.61m) gauge of the Tasmanian Government Railways (1909) and for the Darjeeling Himalayan Railway in India (1911). The Garratt locomotive therefore started life as an engine used almost exclusively on narrow-gauge railways in mountainous regions, but soon developed into a massive type whose basic features generally included outside cylinders with Walschaert valve gear and, with the exception of the Tasmanian unit, simple rather than compound expansion. In South Africa the Garratt locomotives of the GL and GMAM classes were outstandingly effective in terms of performance and reliability, and their availability in significant numbers successfully

A 2-10-2 South American locomotive. Many South American countries, lacking an indigenous manufacturing industry, relied on imports, particularly from America.

there were many attempts to create an effective type of articulated boiler, with two sections connected in the centre by a bellows arrangement, but the technical difficulties of such an arrangement were beyond practical solution.

The Mallet locomotive also appeared in other parts of the world, although only in smaller numbers and to smaller sizes. British companies built such locomotives for operators in Burma, China and South Africa; several French companies built and used the type on the domestic railway network; and in Germany the Maffei company produced Mallet-type locomotives for service with the Royal Bavarian state railway, the Royal

Hungarian state railway and also, in broad-gauge forms, the Central Aragon and Zafra-Huelva railways of Spain.

British industry was responsible for another classic type of articulated locomotive, which was so extensively and successfully operated in many parts of the world at a later date that the Americans, who in fact never adopted the type, came to call it the British Mallet even though it was really the Beyer-Garratt, so named for its designer, Herbert Garratt, an Englishman who lived in Australia and created the first such articulated locomotive in 1909, and the Beyer, Peacock Company that was based in Manchester and later bought Garratt's patents. The Beyer-

No.2098, a German 03-class 4-6-2.

overcame many of the difficulties that had previously afflicted the railroad operations of this important exporter of raw materials and precious metals.

The Beyer-Garratt was not the only type of articulated locomotive to see service in the first quarter of the 20th century. There was also the Meyer type that first appeared in Belgium during 1873 with origins stretching to an earlier time: this possessed two motor bogies, with the leading unit on a spherical pivot and the trailing unit on transverse members, to carry one large boiler. The main frames were those of the motor units, which therefore carried the couplers, and the boiler supported the tanks. The Meyer type of locomotive began to gain real acceptance only in the 1890s after the type was recommended by Robert Stirling for use on the Anglo-Chilean Nitrate Company's railway. In this British-developed model the boiler, tanks and bunker were installed on two parallel girders with their ends resting on the bogies or trucks. Used for the movement of nitrates to the Chilean coast, the locomotives coped well with a railway route including a 1/25 gradient and small-radius curves. The same type of locomotive was used with considerable success on Argentinian and Chilean narrow-gauge railways across the Andes mountains and also, in a considerably broader gauge, on the ore-carrying routes of southern Spain.

Other articulated steam locomotives of the period included not only the original type of Fairlie but also the so-called Modified Fairlie and the Maffei-built Garratt Union, both owing much to the Garratt, and the Hagan which had two sets of coupled wheels and included drive to the rear set. The Hagan was manufactured for the Imperial Prussian state railroad in 1893, and also for the Tasmanian government.

Despite the freight-hauling success of Mallet locomotives in North America, Garratt locomotives in Africa, Meyer locomotives in South America, and the older Fairlie locomotive in Mexico, the only type to gain any success in the passenger locomotive role was the Garratt, and even so the articulated locomotive never found acceptance in several other parts of the world. As a result, many railways stuck with the standard pattern of locomotive in which a rigid framework was carried on the track by wheels on several axles

and itself supported the rest of the locomotive's workings. As noted above, the 0-10-0 locomotive was most favoured in central and eastern Europe in countries such as Austria-Hungary, Germany (most notably Prussia and Bavaria), Italy, Sweden and, most significantly of all, Russia. In this last nation

an excellent design was introduced just before the outbreak of World War I, and this was eventually to be manufactured in numbers running into several thousands, especially as an all-purpose type in the immensely troubled period after the revolution of November 1917 had turned Tsarist Russia into the communist

In Africa, as in many parts of the world, specialized trains haul coal to stoke the fires of industry.

103

A log train hauled by an 0-8-0 heading towards Chai He, China.

U.S.S.R.: many of the locomotives were also manufactured in Sweden by Nydqvist and Helm, and in Germany by companies such as Vulkan and Humboldt. Such was the basic simplicity and reliability of the design that few changes were ever needed, and the type served the U.S.S.R. long and faithfully.

In North America, the 0-10-0 layout was used only as a heavy switcher in the great freight yards. For main-line freight-hauling operations the Americans preferred the locomotive of the 2-10-2 type whose bogies or trucks provided a better ride on the road than any locomotive of the wholly rigid type. The locomotive of 2-10-0 layout was much appreciated in Europe, especially in Austria-Hungary and in the Balkans, where the type's success led to its additional use for express

Norfolk & Western-class Y6B articulated locomotive No.2185, being assembled at the Roanoke yard in May 1949.

A narrow-gauge locomotive hauls sugar cane to a mill in Java.

passenger services. Though it did see a measure of passenger service, the 2-10-0 locomotive was best suited to freight operations, and it was in this role that classic locomotives, such as the 2-10-0 type designed by J.B. Flamme for the Belgian state railroad in the 1920s, gained a considerable reputation. Other classic 2-10-0 locomotives were produced in Austria-Hungary, which was in many respects the ablest European exponent of the large steam locomotive, but the 2-10-0 layout also formed the basis for

expanded locomotives including 2-12-0 units produced in small numbers in Austria-Hungary and Württemberg, and later by France, where the A1 class of 2-12-0 locomotives was built for the nationalized railroad system from 1948. For heavy freight purposes, though, the locomotive with a long rigid wheelbase was basically inferior to the locomotive with articulated groupings of wheels, such as the Mallet and Garratt types. In overall terms, therefore, the very long coupled wheelbase did not survive long, even

though the death throes of the type were extended by final experiments such as the classically huge 4-14-4 locomotive produced in the U.S.S.R. during 1934 for evaluation against an even more substantial Beyer-Garratt 4-8-2+2-8-4 locomotive obtained from the U.K.

In the years up to 1914, the majority of British main-line companies had ordered or constructed some 2-8-0 freight locomotives. These included the Great Western Railway, which had a sizeable fleet of 2800-class locomotives and nine large-wheeled 4700-class 2-8-0 locomotives. The Great Northern Railway, under the technical supervision of Nigel Gresley, designed some successful standard 2-8-0 locomotives for heavy coal and freight traffic from the north-east of England to London. Perhaps the best known type of British heavy freight locomotive of the Edwardian era was the Robinson ROD (Railway Operating Division) 2-8-0 locomotive, many of which were constructed for use by the British army in World War I. After the establishment of the London & North Eastern Railway in 1923, Gresley designed the P1 class of 2-8-2 locomotives to undertake heavy freight work from London

on what had recently been the Great Northern Railway's main line. By a paradoxical turn of events, these locomotives were too successful in technical terms as their considerable power meant that especial care had to be taken to avoid breaking the couplings of the small two-axle coal and goods wagons then in use. Probably the best and certainly the most successful type of locomotive ever designed in the U.K. for the heavy freight role was the Sir William Stanier 8F-class 2-8-0 unit, which was manufactured for the London, Midland & Scottish Railway in the period between 1937 and 1944. So successful was the type that the War Office also ordered many batches for its own

purposes, which included operations in many parts of the world, especially in the Middle East and Persia (now Iran), where trains hauled by 8F-class locomotives were importantly operated to deliver Allied war matériel to the forces and industries of the U.S.S.R. across Persia's northern frontier after the goods had reached the region by ship.

By the 1880s the main railroad operators in all parts of continental Europe, eastern, central and western, were heavily involved in the development, manufacture and large-scale introduction of locomotives of steadily increasing size and capability for the operation of heavy freight services and, to a somewhat lesser extent, mixed traffic services. Among

An Argentine narrow-gauge steam locomotive hauls a mixed load. In South America, the introduction of diesel power was sometimes limited because of the cost of imported diesel fuel relative to locally-mined coal.

A Union Pacific
articulated Big Boy-class
4-8-8-4 hauling a string of
PFE cars through Echo
Canyon, Utah in the early
1950s. The first locomotive
of this type was built in
1941.

China's coal train network is highly developed. Here, a double-headed train wends its way to Gantang.

the first to come to a full appreciation of the benefits offered by such locomotives were several of the larger state railroad organizations of the German empire. When, in the aftermath of Germany's defeat in World War I, the new German republic decided to create a national railroad system by amalgamating the various private and state-owned railroads into the Deutsche Reichsbahn during 1922, the already existing process of developing and manufacturing standard classes, generally based on Prussian designs with a measure of input from the railroad practices of Bavaria and

Württemberg, was expanded to include 2-8-0, 2-10-0 and 2-10-2T type locomotives in large numbers. The French railroad operators had drawn major benefit from locomotive construction during World War I, and also from the import of 140C-class 2-8-0 and American-built Pershing-type 2-8-0 locomotives. This process was repeated after World War II, when the Société Nationale des Chemins de Fer further benefited with the acquisition of 141R-class 2-8-2 locomotives as part of the Marshall Aid plan designed by General George C. Marshall to help Europe recover its economic feet.

By the end of the 20th century's first decade, American railway companies had developed a large network of services operating, among other things, an increasing volume of the freight that represented on the one hand the raw materials needed for the rapidly continuing development of American industrialization and on the other hand finished goods for domestic consumption or for export from the country's large numbers of major sea ports. Thus the design and construction of the latest generation of efficient heavy locomotives to haul these freight trains was of huge importance. A

A South American 2-10-2 locomotive steams past another freight train at Rio Gallegos.

number of the larger railroad companies themselves developed locomotives to meet the need. The Union Pacific Railroad in particular produced two classes of locomotives of outstanding design. These were the Challenger and the Big Boy. Both types were developed from the late 1930s and construction continued until the late 1940s. The Big Boy, designed by Alco and built to the extent of 25 4000-class locomotives, can be regarded as one of the last, and therefore definitive, types of huge steam locomotives for heavy freight haulage purposes. These were the last heavy freight locomotives in service on the Union Pacific Railroad, and the locomotives were not withdrawn until 1959.

The Norfolk & Western Railroad, which operated heavy coal trains in Virginia, possessed a large fleet of Y6B and A class articulated locomotives of the Mallet type, and these too were notable for the superb service they provided from the early 1930s to 1960, when they were finally retired from service as the last steam locomotives used in the U.S.A. for the hauling of heavy freight trains.

Picture Acknowledgements
Ann Ronan at Image Select: pages 10 all, 11 both, 13, 14 above and below, 16 both
*Association of American Railroads: pages 9, 98
*Burlington Northern Railroad: page 2
*Canadian National Railway: page 25 above
*Colourviews: 33
*Delaware & Hudson Railroad: page 8
*Holloway College: page 3
Military Archive & Research Services: pages 27 above, 32, 81, 92, 97, 102
*Nelson Gallery, Atkins Museum: pages 4–5
*New Zealand Railways: page 90
*Norfolk & Western Railroad: page 105
*Northern Pacific Railroad: pages 6–7, 20 above right
Railfotos, Millbrook House Limited: cover pages, pages 15, 17, 18, 19, 20 above left and below, 21, 23, 24 both, 25 below, 27 below, 28, 29, 30, 31, 34, 35 (P. Harris), 37, 38, 39, 40 both, 41, 42, 43, 44, 45, 46, 47, 48, 49, 50 both, 51, 52, 53, 54, 56, 57, 58, 59, 60, 61, 62, 63, 64, 65, 66, 67, 69, 70, 71, 72, 74–75: (pages 76 both, 77, 78 both, 79, 80 both, 82, 107 P.B.Whitehouse): 83, 84, 85, 86, 87, 88, 89, 93, 95, 96, 99, 100, 101, 103, 104, 106, 109, 110
*Science Museum, London: page 12 both
*Union Pacific Railroad Museum: pages 22, 26, 36, 94, 108
*Victorian Railways: page 91

*Prints supplied through Military Archive & Research Services, England.